Looking After Children: Assessing Outcomes in Child Care

The Report of an Independent
Working Party established by
the Department of Health

Edited by

Roy Parker (Chairperson)

Harriet Ward (Academic Secretary)

Sonia Jackson

Jane Aldgate

Peter Wedge

London: HMSO

Applications for reproduction should be made to HMSO's Copyright Unit
First published 1991
Fourth impression 1995

ISBN 0 11 321459 6

Contents

iii

Members of the Department of Health Working Party on Child Care Outcomes

Dr Jane Aldgate

Lecturer in Applied Social Studies and Fellow of St. Hilda's College
Department of Applied Social Studies and Social Research
University of Oxford

Mr Roger Bullock

Senior Research Fellow
Dartington Social Research Unit
University of Bristol

Dr Carolyn Davies

Research Management Division
Department of Health

Mrs Sonia Jackson

Senior Lecturer in Social Work
Department of Social Work
University of Bristol

Professor Martin Knapp

Deputy Director
Personal Social Services Research Unit
University of Kent at Canterbury

Mr Peter McCoy

Principal Planning Officer
Social Services Department
Suffolk County Council

Professor Roy Parker
(Chairperson)

Research Professor in Social Administration
Department of Social Policy & Social Planning
University of Bristol

Professor Barbara Tizard — Emeritus Professor in Education
Thomas Coram Research Unit
Institute of Education
University of London

Professor John Triseliotis — Director of Social Work Education
Department of Social Policy &
Social Work
University of Edinburgh

Dr Harriet Ward
(Academic Secretary) — Research Associate
Department of Social Policy &
Social Planning
University of Bristol

Professor Peter Wedge — Director
Social Work Development Unit
University of East Anglia

Note

The implementation of the Children Act 1989 introduces changes in terminology. The term 'in care' now refers solely to children who are subject to care orders. Children who are cared for on a voluntary basis are 'accommodated' by the local authority. Both the group of children in care and those who are accommodated are 'looked after' by the local authority, or 'looked after away from home'. In this book we have also used 'in care', in quotation marks, to refer to the whole population of children who would formerly have been covered by that term, whatever their legal status.

Preface

This book is part of the Department of Health initiative on the assessment of child care outcomes. The complete project is published by HMSO, and consists of three items:

Looking After Children: Assessment and Action Records
This is a series of six schedules designed to measure children's progress and assess the quality of care they receive from babyhood to eighteen years. The schedules can be used to make assessments for any child, but they are particularly relevant for monitoring the care of children who are supervised or looked after by local authorities or who are living apart from their families in hospitals, special schools or other residential accommodation. These records can be used either separately or as a means of reviewing children's cases on a regular basis. As well as the *Assessment and Action Records* the complete package for use in reviews contains formats for making plans, for conducting statutory reviews of children's cases and for collecting basic data. All have been designed to meet the requirements of the Children Act 1989.

The assessment and action records were developed by Harriet Ward, Sonia Jackson, Jane Aldgate, Carolyn Davies, Roy Parker and Barbara Tizard. Additional advice on health issues was given by Dr Alan Emond from the Institute of Child Health, University of Bristol. The record for older children was devised in consultation with Jane Rowe, and owes much to the *Ready to Cope Alone* checklist which was being constructed during the same period. In finalising the content of the schedules the authors had the benefit of advice from Dr Walter Barker of the

Early Childhood Development Unit, University of Bristol; from Dr Lumsden Walker; from representatives of Black and in Care; from the Family Rights Group; from the National Foster Care Association; and from the social workers and residential staff in the five local authorities which participated in the initial pilot study. Young people 'in care' and their parents were also consulted.

Looking After Children: Guidelines for Users of the Assessment and Action Records
This is a short guide which introduces practitioners to the schedules and explains why formal assessments are necessary, and how they should be undertaken. Step-by-step instructions are given for completing the forms. Brief information suggesting which data are most appropriate for analysis is also included. The guidelines were written by Harriet Ward, in consultation with Alan Emond, Sonia Jackson and Roy Parker.

Towards a computerised system
Plans to produce a computer programme which can be used in place of the written records were first initiated by Peter McCoy. As well as serving all the purposes that the written materials fulfil, computerisation will facilitate analysis of the aggregated information as it is collected. It will be possible to produce a flexible system which can be adjusted to meet local requirements. Work on the production of a comprehensive computer-based version of the complete *Looking After Children* package: the assessment and action records, the subsidiary forms for making plans, conducting reviews and collecting basic data, and guidance for users, is currently in process. Further enquiries should be addressed to Dr Harriet Ward, Department of Social Policy and Social Planning, University of Bristol.

Looking After Children: Assessing Outcomes in Child Care: the Report of an Independent Working Party established by the Department of Health, edited by Roy Parker (Chairperson), Harriet Ward, Sonia Jackson, Jane Aldgate and Peter Wedge.

This book is intended for those who wish to pursue further the wider issues involved in constructing outcome measures in child care. It explores the elusive concept of outcome in work with children and provides a theoretical foundation for the development of further research on outcome measures in other fields. It also explains the theoretical basis for the assessment and action records, and describes the process by which they were developed. However, it can be read independently from the rest of the 'Looking After Children' project.

The book is based mainly on written and oral contributions from members of the Department of Health Working Party on Child Care Outcomes. However, the working party also had the advantage of advice and comments from a number of other people, many of whom were present at the original outcomes meeting. These include Dorothy Whitaker, Michael Power, Michael Little and Anthony Maluccio. A small group of the working party was formed to take forward the editing of this rich material. They were Roy Parker, Harriet Ward, Sonia Jackson, Jane Aldgate and Peter Wedge. However, in its final form the book reflects the views of the working party as a whole, and all its members take responsibility for the ideas and opinions expressed in it.

We would like to thank Patricia Crates and Patricia Lees for their secretarial assistance and general support.

We are grateful to the Department of Health for setting up the Working Party, providing the funds for it to meet over an extended period, and supporting the continuing research; we would particularly like to thank Carolyn Davies, our liaison officer, for her consistent encouragement and active participation in the project.

We also thank the Dartington Social Research Unit, the Thomas Coram Research Unit and the School of Applied Social Studies, University of Bristol, for providing a variety of facilities and for their continuing interest and support.

Chapter 1

Introduction: Why Assess Outcomes?

I   The Background

The second half of the nineteenth century saw the establishment of an array of children's services and child protection legislation. It was an age of moral confidence that sprang from a mixture of religious revivalism and a belief in the essential pliability of children once exposed to new environments that separated them from the deleterious influences of what were frequently regarded as feckless, neglectful and worthless families. In that climate doubts about the rightness of such social interventions were few and far between; and if what was being done in the interests of the child was self-evidently right the question of whether it actually led to desirable outcomes was hardly likely to be asked.

Much of that nineteenth century confidence survived well into the twentieth century. Indeed, it only began to be seriously undermined from the 1960s onwards. Several factors conspired to effect that change.

First, researchers began to investigate a variety of social conditions. The Social Science Research Council was established in the early 1960s and the rapid expansion of higher education during the same period saw the creation of many new departments of social policy, sociology and social work in the universities and polytechnics. A spate of social science research followed, much of it devoted to the exploration of poverty, deprivation and structural inequality. This raised doubts about the belief in the onward march of social improvement. It was in this more critical atmosphere that the first systematic studies of

1

child care policy and practice were undertaken. A number of researchers endeavoured to assess the 'success' of particular policies, most notably foster care (Trasler, 1960; Parker, 1966; George, 1970). Although this policy had been vigorously encouraged since the Children Act 1948, disturbingly high rates of failure were reported. It could no longer be taken for granted that foster care was inevitably superior to other provisions for disadvantaged children; the question remained open. Indeed it led to consideration of wider issues such as whether it might not be better for most vulnerable children to remain with their families: did separation really improve their life chances? Such questions were vividly highlighted in 1973 by Rowe and Lambert in their publication *Children Who Wait*. Many children were shown to be languishing in 'care' with scant attention being paid to contacts with their families and with no firm plans for their futures. The study was extremely influential, not least amongst practitioners.

With the support of, for instance, the Department of Health and the Economic and Social Research Council, a substantial body of research has now been undertaken in the field of child care. However, as the results of successive studies have unfolded, they have revealed shortcomings of various kinds, both in policy and in practice (see Kahan, 1989 and Sinclair, 1988). The research has contributed to a growing disquiet about the quality and appropriateness of services for disadvantaged children, and has emphasised the number of needs that have not been met.

A second factor that has weakened the previous certainties in child care has been the emergence of the idea of 'prevention'. From the Children and Young Persons Act 1963 onwards it has been possible for local authorities to spend money on measures intended to diminish the need for children to come into 'care' or be brought before the courts. Again, progress has been uneven, and it has been far from easy to determine what are the exact requirements of effective 'prevention'. Nevertheless, new resources aimed at keeping children with their families rather than at keeping them apart, have been made available. The increasing prominence given to 'prevention' has emphasised that there *is* an alternative to looking after children away from

2

home, and has thereby created a policy option against which 'care' arrangements can be compared. In that way, the option of 'prevention' has been instrumental in intensifying the principal dilemma that is now widely recognised to exist in child care policy; namely, whether children who are presumed to be 'at risk' of one kind or another should or should not be removed from home. Yet we cannot begin to resolve this dilemma until we know how vulnerable children and their families respond to different courses of action.

A similar set of issues has been uncovered by the more recent policy emphasis upon restoring children to their families as soon as possible, rather than allowing them to remain 'in care' for long periods. In particular, children who have been committed to care by the courts have increasingly been returned home 'on trial' without the order having been discharged (Farmer and Parker, 1991). When children in this situation are re-abused, questions naturally arise about the relative merits of keeping children 'in care' or allowing them home. Such matters cannot be resolved without knowing which children, under which circumstances, can be safely restored to their families.

Yet another factor has severely undermined both public and professional confidence in our child care services. Since the inquiry into the death of Maria Colwell in 1973, there have been well over forty similar investigations. Not all have involved a child's death or been concerned with tragedies that have occurred in children's own homes. All, however, have produced profound disquiet and have made it plain that public supervision or 'care' can provide no guarantee that a child's well-being will be safeguarded, even at the most basic level. One cannot avoid asking how far the events that have triggered off the stream of inquiries represent merely the tip of the iceberg.

There is no doubt that such failures in the child care system existed before Maria Colwell's death, but remained hidden. Their public exposure, through official inquiries, has been accompanied by a growing, though still under-expressed, concern on the part of parents and children involved in the system,

3

to be given better information about what happens. Their demands for greater participation can be regarded as part of the consumer movement in general, but have undoubtedly been encouraged and facilitated by pressure groups such as the National Association of Young People in Care, the Family Rights Group and the Parents' Association.

The 1970s witnessed a rapid rise in the number of children 'in care', with a parallel increase in expenditure on the related services. Although the number declined steadily in the 1980s a variety of other factors operated to sustain expenditure levels— most notably the rise in public concern about child protection and the proliferation of regulations and guidelines aimed at ensuring that omissions in social work or administrative practice did not lead to unnecessary risk and suffering. The 'cost question' has been yet another influence in promoting a greater preoccupation with standards of performance, with obtaining 'value for money' and with the efficient management of services (Department of the Environment, District Audit, 1981). However, none of these issues can be satisfactorily addressed unless we have some clear idea of how far each of the various child care services has succeeded in increasing the long-term well-being of children.

Thus, the conjunction of several forces has led to an increasing concern about 'outcomes' in child care. However, as we shall see later in the book, these outcomes are difficult to specify, identify and measure. None of these tasks is straightforward; yet all must be confronted if we are to take seriously the question of accountability. The efficient expenditure of public funds should not be the only consideration; of even greater importance are the needs of those families which encounter serious difficulties in their efforts to bring up children. Thankfully, it now seems to be regarded as axiomatic that outcomes are important: there remains, however the problem of how they are to be identified and measured, both in research and in practice.

II   A Working Party

It was in this climate of unease, coupled with an acknowledged need for better information, that the (then) Department of Health and Social Security suggested that a working party be set up to consider the question of outcomes in child care. Leading child care researchers in Britain were invited to meet for two days at Dartington Hall in Devon to present the results of their own past and current experience and to establish the state of knowledge in the field. They moved on to discuss and analyse the concept of outcome and to consider how it might be assessed. A list of the people who attended this meeting is included in Appendix One.

This first meeting brought together a remarkable range and depth of experience on the subject of children supervised or looked after by local authorities. Nevertheless, it became apparent that, with few exceptions, almost everything that could be called 'outcomes research' centred on a single measure—the breakdown or continuance of placements. On many of the aspects of a child's life that are generally agreed to be important, for example education whilst 'in care', no research existed at all. It further became clear that no satisfactory measures or assessment instruments were available for determining outcomes for children who had been or were being looked after by local authorities. Practitioners were just as ill-equipped as were researchers. Furthermore, the information on social work intervention that was available in social services departments or elsewhere was rarely geared to the assessment of outcomes and therefore could not be used conveniently for that purpose. Moreover, as the discussion proceeded, it became evident that the very idea of an outcome, which had seemed fairly clear at the outset, presented great difficulties as soon as an attempt was made to apply it. The apparently straightforward but enormously important question of what happens to children who grow up or spend part of their lives 'in care' was not easily answered. For example, the effects of what happens to a child during a period 'in care', or what happens to a family as a result of social work intervention, are not readily disentangled from the effects of other influences that lie quite outside the power of social services departments to control. Furthermore, how can the experiences of children who have spent their whole lives in residential or foster homes be compared with those who have lived 'in care' for only a few months? At what point are we justified in describing an event, or a stage reached, as an outcome? And supposing that we could recognise an outcome when we saw one, how should it be assessed and evaluated?

A number of those present agreed to continue meeting in order to wrestle with these and many of the other issues that emerged from these first discussions. Their ultimate purpose was to see what could be done to develop a practical scheme for assessing outcomes. Although the information and ideas that were shared during the initial meeting provided an invaluable basis for the subsequent discussion, this book draws principally upon the deliberations of, and the papers prepared for, the smaller working party. Chapters 2 to 5 review the conceptual and theoretical questions that surround the identification and assessment of outcomes. Chapters 6 and 7 reflect the work undertaken by the five members of the working party who took on the more specific task of designing outcome measures that could be used by both practitioners and researchers. Naturally, those measures (examples of which are included in the appendix) have drawn upon the work of the whole group. The final chapter describes how these instruments were piloted and discusses some of the preliminary findings that emerged from research on their application.

III   Recent Developments

The National Context
Of course the child care services did not stand still during the three years that the working party met and the outcome measures were being developed. In fact it was a time when accepted ideas were being increasingly challenged and when far-reaching legislative changes were being introduced through the Children Act 1989. This was officially and fairly described

as 'the most comprehensive piece of legislation which Parliament has ever enacted about children' (Department of Health, 1989a). Indeed, it came exactly 100 years after the first major children's legislation, much of which had re-appeared in only a slightly different guise in the many Acts and regulations that were passed in the intervening years. The 1989 Act marks a significant break with this tradition. It is intended to usher in a fundamental rethinking of the whole purpose and conduct of local authority activity concerned with the welfare of children, exceeding in its scale and depth the major transformations that followed from the Children Act 1948.

The 1989 Act stimulated a surge of activity in the child care field. Nearly all local authorities appointed specialist staff to plan its implementation in October, 1991. New initiatives in training were taken and study packs and conferences abounded. In addition to the wealth of official guidance on implementation, all the major voluntary children's organisations responded energetically to the opportunities and challenges that the Act presents.

Since the whole exercise of which this book is a product was carried out in close consultation and in active co-operation with the Department of Health, it both influenced and was influenced by the thinking behind the Act; and the later stages of the work were informed by the necessity for any measures which we designed to mesh with the requirements of the new legislation and assist local authorities in its implementation.

The emphasis which the Act places upon monitoring underlined the need for a soundly-based method of setting goals and assessing outcomes, particularly in conducting six-monthly reviews. Although reviews on children in foster care have been required since 1955, and on all children who are the responsibility of local authorities since 1969, the way in which this was done had been left to the discretion of individual departments. This has led to considerable variations in what actually happens. Furthermore, although the need for reviews is widely agreed, they can easily degenerate into a formality that makes little impact on the children whom they are supposed to be helping. The absence of a standard agenda may contribute to this as does the brevity of many reviews, which allows no possibility for important areas of a child's life to be addressed in any depth. For example, Sinclair found that half of the six-monthly reviews carried out in the area offices which she studied lasted ten minutes or less (Sinclair, 1984). Sometimes little preparation had been done, so that important information was missing; the aims and proposed actions were expressed in such general terms that, later on, it was impossible to tell if they had been realised or not. Often the only matter discussed was whether the child or young person should move or stay in the same placement.

It is clearly the intention of the 1989 Act that reviews should be much more serious and searching exercises, and many local authorities have already made progress in this direction. To be productive, a review needs to have a clear frame of reference, a way of assessing what has happened since the last review, a means of reconsidering objectives and then of deciding whether they have been achieved. In chapter 6, we suggest that this requires the systematic monitoring of a child's development over a range of different dimensions together with a clear understanding of the aims.

A second important issue that is highlighted by the Children Act 1989 and which was already in the forefront of the working party's thinking, is the need to ensure that the views of children, their caregivers and their families are taken into account both in determining what should be done (and by whom) and in assessing what has happened. After all, there is likely to be a variety of perceptions regarding what outcomes are, what shaped them and how they should be assessed. A single social work opinion is unlikely to give a complete picture and, indeed, the views of those involved may be irreconcilable.

It was for reasons such as these that we made provision for the outcome measures described in chapter 7 to be completed by the social worker in collaboration with the direct caregiver and with the child or young person, and to be shared with parents and other family members if appropriate. The early findings of the research reported in chapter 8 indicate that, with sensitive handling, this can be experienced by parents, caregivers and young people as an important and enjoyable undertaking rather than as an intrusion.

A third question was thrown into prominence by the Children Act 1989. When considering child care outcomes, what is the relevant population whose experiences should be assessed? While safeguarding the right of the child to protection from ill-treatment, the Act redefines and blurs the boundaries between parental responsibility and State intervention. The risks and costs, both human and financial, of separating children from their families are fully recognised, but the Act also makes clear that to keep children out of 'care' should not be the overriding objective if this means that they and their families do not get the help that they need. The Act aims to establish a new image of local authority child care services as supportive rather than punitive. Thus, the administrative category of 'in care' is abolished, except for those subject to a court order. Children are 'accommodated' or 'looked after' on a voluntary basis by a local authority in order to help a family in difficulties. Both their parents retain responsiblity for them and have the right to be kept closely informed and consulted about their care and well-being. Thus the Act provides a framework within which a much higher level of support can be given to children and parents without the stigmatising and divisive effect of a formal reception into 'care'.

However, this new approach does also remove the spurious clarity that the old system provided. Whereas it might have been argued that local authorities had a special obligation to those children to whom they stood in the position of parent, and lesser responsibility for those whose families social workers were merely advising and befriending, that distinction can no longer be sustained. Now that it is not possible to fall back on a convenient administrative categorization it is less obvious for precisely which children it is appropriate to design and apply outcome measures. This question is discussed in chapter 5.

The International Context

The period during which the working party met was also a time when increasing attention was given to the needs of children worldwide. In November, 1989, the General Assembly of the United Nations adopted the Convention on the Rights of the Child and in September, 1990, the World Summit for Children took place in New York. Even if the latter event did not altogether fulfil the hopes that it raised, it did at least confirm an important position for children on the international agenda.

By comparison with the child prostitutes of Bangkok, the street children of Brazil or the abandoned babies in Romanian institutions (Reich, 1990) even the most deprived British child might seem well off. But, whatever the point from which they start, governments and child welfare agencies grapple with the same problems of how best to support and facilitate the task of childrearing or provide substitutes for parents who, for whatever reasons, cannot give satisfactory care. The Convention on the Rights of the Child sets a standard which is far from being achieved even in an advanced industrial society like our own. The systematic monitoring of outcomes should enable government and local authorities to identify where action needs to be taken to ensure that all British children enjoy the rights specified by the Convention.

Child care research and practice in Britain, despite its reference to American literature, has tended in the past to be rather insular in outlook, an attitude perhaps epitomised by our insistence on using our own term (child care) for what everybody else calls 'child welfare'. However, we are becoming increasingly aware of the importance of taking an international perspective and of the valuable lessons to be learnt from cross-national research. Several members of the working party presented papers at an international conference on Services for Children and Youth where the ideas on assessment of outcomes developed in this book were shown to have considerable relevance to researchers and practitioners from other countries (Hudson and Galaway, 1990).

IV   The Uses of Outcome Measurement

While the importance of outcome measures to researchers is self-evident, many other groups of people need to know much more than they can at present about the consequences of child care decisions, the influence of agency policy on the lives of individual children and the effect of the experiences that they are offered. These include children themselves and their families, social workers, foster carers, residential staff, social services managers, advisers and policy-makers, teachers and trainers.

It might be argued that parents have the paramount right to information about outcomes and have been the people least likely to get it. Children are looked after by local authorities because their families are not able to meet their needs and are obliged to ask for help, or because these families are deemed to be incapable of providing good enough care. Either way parents are entitled to evidence that the job is being done better than they could have done it themselves.

A common complaint of parents in the past was that they were not kept informed even of quite significant events in the lives of the children who were separated from them. Under the provisions of the Children Act 1989 this should no longer happen. Local authorities have a clear duty to maintain contact with parents. Yet in the absence of any guidelines on assessing outcome what are they to tell them? How can parents know if a social services department is doing a good job or not? It should also be remembered that parents are not the only people concerned. Other relatives, such as grandparents, aunts, uncles, even longstanding family friends may, as the Act recognises, have a legitimate interest in outcomes and a contribution to make.

The children themselves are another group whose right to know is undeniable. When Graham Gaskin demanded to know what quality of care had been provided for him during his childhood innumerable obstacles were put in his way and he was forced to take legal action in order to obtain access to his files (MacVeigh, 1982). In these days of open records he might have found it easier to obtain information but just as hard to make sense of what happened to him and the reasons for the actions of the social services department. This is a recurrent theme in the recollections of people who have spent time 'in care', especially when they feel that life has not gone well for them.

Social workers need outcome measures to fulfil their obligation to act as a channel of communication between social services departments and families, but they also urgently need better information in order to become more aware of the impact of their own actions and decisions. Otherwise there is a risk that they will not formulate explicit objectives or follow them through systematically (Knapp, Bryson and Lewis, 1985). They then have no way of assessing the effectiveness of their practice and thereby improving it. There is no basis for them, or others, to learn from their experience. It was for this reason that the working party attached particular importance to designing a form of outcome measurement that would assist social workers in the case management of individual children.

Rather than scales or tests, which might reduce the social worker's role in the assessment of outcome to that of a collector of data, we have produced an assessment and action record that is designed to have a direct influence on practice. As explained more fully in chapters 6 and 7, the schedules (adapted to the age of the child) specify objectives derived from research on child development and child care practice and link them to actions which have been shown to be necessary for their achievement. In particular they focus on what needs to be done at certain stages or times in a child's life.

The assessment and action records are intended to assist frontline practitioners in three ways: first, by helping them to clarify their aims and to identify potential areas of concern; secondly, by enabling them to make better-informed decisions and to take a more comprehensive view of planning for individual children, and thirdly by focusing their attention on the information that should be obtained in the interest of the child.

The need to set objectives and assess outcomes does not stop at the individual practitioner. Team leaders and managers also require a means of checking the quality of work carried out, spotting omissions and identifying training needs. Even if the team leader has specialist knowledge of child development, which cannot be assumed, important elements can easily be overlooked without the support of a well-constructed scheme of assessment.

An assessment and action record of the kind that we propose also has great potential for use in supervision, with its dual function of ensuring accountability and encouraging professional development (Parsloe, 1981). It provides an effective way of checking if agreed actions have been carried out; but it also links action to outcome, a stage often omitted in the discussion of social work cases. If decisions and actions in line with received opinion and agency policy do not produce good results for the child this should prompt some useful questioning.

Another advantage of adopting standard measures of outcome is that they create consistency in the collection of information so that all casepapers contain comparable data, making it possible to examine a particular area such as, for example, the development of self-care skills, across a number of different cases. It will be much easier then for supervisors to encourage social workers to look at common factors as well as at children's individual characteristics, and to think what the implications might be for policy and for their own practice. Scrutinising outcomes in this way may suggest unexpected connections and could open up interesting possibilities for practitioner research.

The value of using a standardised form of outcome assessment in child care case reviews has already been mentioned. The assessment and action record that we have designed ensures that important areas of development are considered, not only the question of placement. The use of the outcome measures in case reviews is further discussed in chapter 8.

At higher management levels, where judgments have to be made about the efficiency and effectiveness of child care services in relation to costs, reliable, consistent information on outcomes is essential. Without it, forms of provision or practices which do not contribute to children's welfare may continue simply because they already exist, when the same resources could be used in a more effective way (Knapp, 1989). The aggregation of data from assessment and action records can lead to the identification of unmet needs and point to areas where new policies are required.

The results of outcome research have an important part to play in enabling the teachers and trainers of social workers to test and evaluate the information, perspectives and theories about work with children that they offer to students. The system of case monitoring that is proposed in this book should be particularly useful for these purposes, stimulating questions about goal-setting and values at one level and questions about the whole purpose of the child care service at another. The assessment instrument that has emerged as a distillation of the working party's deliberations links specific social work or care inputs to desirable outcomes and thereby demonstrates, more directly than is usually possible, the interrelationships between theory, research and practice.

Finally we hope that the system of outcome assessment which has evolved from our work will make it easier to monitor the effect of the new Children Act on the lives of the children and young people whom it is intended to benefit, both by facilitating and simplifying the work of researchers and by enabling practitioners to play a more active role in a variety of research initiatives.

Researching the Outcome Measures
Having negotiated the transition between the theoretical deliberations of the working party and the task of devising an assessment instrument based on the principles established, the next step was to test them in practice. It was decided at this stage to produce monitoring schedules for two age groups only, three to four and over sixteen year-olds. These age bands were regarded as particularly significant— just before starting school and around the time of leaving care. They would also give a good idea of the suitability of the scheme for use both with young children and with adolescents. Social workers from five

local authorities used the schedules on two occasions to assess a child on their caseload. The object was to test the acceptability of the monitoring instrument from the social worker's point of view and to obtain suggestions for improvements from managers, research staff and front-line practitioners. The findings of the study, completed early in 1991, are reported in chapter 8. They provided a basis for the design and content of the complete range of schedules that are published alongside this book.

Although the number of children involved was relatively small and the purpose of the pilot study was not to record the impact of the schedules upon practice, there were clear indications that the use of a structured monitoring instrument had a benefical effect on social work with children and families in at least two ways. First, it directed social workers' attention to previously overlooked aspects of the child's experience and development. Secondly, it encouraged them to discuss these matters with foster carers, parents and young people themselves, and to listen carefully to their views.

With the support of the Department of Health a more extensive study of the use of the schedules is due to begin in September, 1991. This will enable them to be evaluated more fully and at several different levels. The main questions to be asked are:

1. Does the employment of the assessment and action records improve the quality of service provided and, in turn does this improve the outcome for the child?

2. Can the schedules provide aggregate data about different categories of children and young people throughout an area in order to inform policy, resource allocation and the refinement of theory and practice?

3. Can the information contained in the schedules suggest important questions for research as well as providing readily available source material that will make that research easier to undertake?

A Better Service for Children in Need
Recording and assessing outcome is not a cost-free exercise. Apart from the direct expense of stationery, printing and

computing, it takes time that could be used in other ways. Any particular scheme can only be justified if it can be shown to produce improvements for children and young people looked after or supervised by social services departments, both in their current experience and in their longer term development and prospects as adults. The system of outcome measurement devised by the working party is one possible approach.

The assessment and action records will inevitably be used by more people than will read this book. The records are accompanied by guidelines designed to meet the practical needs of those who will use the schedules in their work, but who do not have time to examine in detail the theories upon which they are based. However, many of those responsible for management, research and policy in child care and other related fields will need to understand fully the arguments and assumptions from which the instrument evolved. We have therefore attempted in the following chapters to set out and explain as clearly as possible the principles which underlie the scheme we propose, and the conceptual problems that have to be overcome however outcomes are to be measured. We do not underestimate the difficulty of the task, but are sure that the attempt must be made. Ultimately, whatever the good intentions of service providers, child welfare agencies can only be judged by the *effect* of their efforts on the people in whose lives they intervene.

Summary of the Main Points from this Chapter

1. When the child care services were first established few doubts were expressed about the appropriateness of social work interventions and the question of assessing outcomes did not arise. Recently, research into modern social conditions, the emergence of theories about prevention, the weakening of confidence in the public care of children following a number of well-documented tragedies, the attention given to consumer views and the emphasis on cost-effectiveness

have all served to produce a climate in which the development of reliable means of assessing outcome is increasingly seen as a necessity.

2. The Department of Health Working Party on Child Care Outcomes was set up in order to consider the issues involved in developing a practical scheme for assessing outcomes for children who are looked after or supervised by local authorities. Their work has been closely aligned with the Children Act 1989 which was being debated and introduced during the period of their discussions. The emphasis placed in the assessment scheme on regular monitoring of children's cases, on sharing decision-making between all those who are responsible for a child's welfare, and on offering services to every child in need, reflect the spirit of the new Act.

3. The measures of outcome that we have designed, the considerations upon which they are based and the preliminary results of a study to test their feasibility will all be described and discussed in later chapters. The scheme of assessment is intended to produce valuable data for researchers and also to have a direct influence on social work practice. It should therefore be of use to all those involved in the public care of children, not only researchers, practitioners, managers and policy-makers, but also parents and children themselves.

Chapter 2

Unravelling the Concept

The idea of an outcome is commonplace. It is embedded in the assumptions about cause and effect that enable us to make sense of our daily lives and the world around us. From the performance of simple mechanical tasks to the more complicated management of affairs there is a widespread conviction that one thing leads to another, that actions have identifiable and anticipated consequences. These consequences are frequently referred to as outcomes: but what are outcomes in child care? The answer is more complex than everyday usage of the term suggests.

To start with there is the question of perspective. Different people think of different events or situations as outcomes. Those that concern social workers reflect the job that they do. The issues addressed by researchers are determined by their particular disciplines as well as by considerations of whether certain occurrences can actually be identified and measured. Likewise, the significance that they and others attach to particular outcomes is affected by the currency of this or that theory. For example, theories of attachment have influenced British child care research but have made little impact on the work carried out in Eastern Europe.

The outcomes of interest to researchers (or to those who fund them) may not be those that are of greatest concern to parents or children. Outcomes that are regarded as significant by professionals may seem to others to be unimportant or incomprehensible. If children or parents feel themselves to be the victims of an uncertain and capricious world then their chief concern may be to avoid the unwelcome outcomes of other people's actions. So much depends upon expectations and standpoints. Many different occurrences and situations can be viewed as outcomes depending upon who is making the judgement, the nature of their involvement and, above all, upon what is considered to be important.

There is a close connection between outcome and evaluation. This is because the purposes of the child care services are conceived mainly in terms of effecting change, whether that be the prevention or the promotion of certain conditions. Indeed, social work interventions in the private sphere of family life can only be justified if it is believed that necessary changes will thereby occur. The success or failure of such interventions is assessed according to whether, say, a child ceases to be abused, is reunited with his or her family or is found a permanent alternative home. In that sense the child care service is outcome-orientated and it is for this reason that the determination and measurement of outcome has been regarded as an integral part of the process of evaluation.

If, in the interests of improving services, the nature of evaluation is to be better understood, and if ways are to be found by which it can be more effectively conducted, then the concept of an 'outcome' has to be unravelled. At the very least a classification has to be made so that distinctions can be drawn between different types of outcomes. Three questions are helpful in approaching this task:

(i)   For whom is something considered to be an outcome?

(ii) Should greater emphasis be given to specific or to general outcomes?

(iii) When are outcomes assumed to occur?

In addition, it is necessary to retain a firm grip on the problem of actually evaluating outcomes once they have been satisfactorily identified. It is also necessary to be aware of the extent to which the technical difficulties of evaluation may lead to the choice of certain circumstances or conditions as significant outcomes rather than others. We introduce some of these technical issues in the next chapter and explore more theoretical matters in chapter 4.

I   Outcomes for Whom?

There are at least five kinds of outcomes in child care that reflect different perspectives and interests. They are:

(i)   Public outcomes

(ii)   Service outcomes

(iii)   Professional outcomes

(iv)   Family outcomes

(v)   Child outcomes

Public Outcomes

Child care interventions are largely publicly organised, publicly financed and made within a framework determined by public statute. Public bodies are held accountable for what happens: there is a range of public expectations about what should be achieved or forestalled. Certainly, these expectations change, are inconsistent and sometimes contradictory: but that does not belie the fact that they exist and, through the activities of the media, exist as powerful political forces. The public has views about which outcomes in child care are to be applauded and, more often, which outcomes are to be deplored, albeit that these opinions are most usually expressed about particular cases rather than about the service as a whole.

An assortment of popular expectations for child care jostle, compete and sometimes conflict with each other; although it is difficult to say which of them predominates, several are in constant circulation. The public wants children protected from a variety of depredations; it wants parents' rights and family life to be safeguarded against unwarranted interference by the State; it wants to be protected from the unwelcome behaviour of older children; and it expects all this to be done quietly, smoothly, efficiently and effectively. These are important elements that determine the broad political framework from which the evaluation of child care cannot be divorced. They influence which outcomes attract most attention.

Service Outcomes

There is a second way of viewing the question 'outcomes for whom?' That is by seeing it from the perspective of social service managers or elected members in the public sector, and management boards in the private or voluntary sectors, all of whom are concerned with the overall performance of an organisation. Of course, they cannot ignore the nature of public expectations or the extent to which legal requirements and local procedures have been followed and proper standards of service maintained; but the outcomes to which they also have to attend are frequently expressed in aggregate terms. For example, they will be concerned about the number and rate of children being looked after by the local authority; the proportion of children in foster homes; upward and downward trends, and unit costs.

Statistics such as these are often interpreted at their face value, with little attention being paid to the reasons behind them or their relationship to other figures. A reduction in the numbers of children being looked after by a local authority is usually regarded as a positive service outcome. Such an evaluation may be justified, for the figures may reflect improved methods of prevention. On the other hand, such a trend may also be associated with, for instance, demographic changes, a reduction in the local authority's ability to meet the needs of children at risk, or an increase in the provision made by other agencies such as the prison service. Statistical trends need to be carefully interpreted if service outcomes are to be accurately evaluated.

Of course, these kinds of 'statistical' outcomes are not what interest the parents or children with whom the services are engaged. Nor are they the kinds of outcomes that attract much attention from, say, backbench MPs or journalists who are more likely to seize upon what they believe to be case scandals. When case scandals occur they, too, are undeniably a crucial outcome for the service organisations, for they are frequently regarded as symptomatic of a more general malaise.

Clearly, social service organizations have to be concerned about both general and individual child care outcomes. Yet these two perspectives are not always compatible, partly because they are different in character but also because they are liable to have different implications for action. They certainly lead to somewhat different ways of conceiving 'outcomes in child care'. It should not be assumed that relevant outcomes for the child care service as a whole can be identified in the same way as outcomes for the individual children whom the service endeavours to help.

Professional Outcomes
A third way of approaching the question of 'outcomes for whom?' is from the professional viewpoint. Child care staff have expectations about what they are trying to achieve. These influence what they consider to be important outcomes. In social work, as in medicine or education, practitioners are mostly concerned with what happens to individual children or families. Exactly what kind of outcomes figure most prominently in their work will depend upon which problems are considered to be most pressing as well as upon how they are understood and interpreted. Outcomes will tend to be seen as a reflection of professional interventions (whether successful or not). In that sense they will be thought of as social work outcomes; that is, outcomes against which social work performance can be judged. The focus, therefore, will be not only on the fact of a child's changed situation but also on the means and the manner by which that change has come about.

Family Outcomes
Child care services impinge upon families. It is, therefore, also reasonable to consider which outcomes may be seen as important for the family as a whole (however that be defined) or for its different members. Nevertheless, it should not be assumed that there are common interests within families. This is apparent in contested custody cases and in the legislative provision for the separate representation of children in care proceedings. Not only may different members of a family attach a different value to the same outcome but they may be more interested in some

outcomes than others, reflecting their different aspirations, intentions and expectations. Choosing to concentrate on an outcome that seems important to one family member may distort any subsequent evaluation of the impact of the child care services. For example, a difficult child may become more disturbed if he or she is removed from home whilst, on the other hand, the rest of the family may benefit. Or a child may flourish in his or her new foster home but the foster carers' own child may become restless and unhappy (Parker, 1966).

Keeping a family intact may be achieved at the expense of a victimised member who continues to be down-trodden or ill-treated. We do not yet know enough about sibling attachments to be certain whether keeping together or reuniting siblings who are frequently in conflict with one another should be regarded as a satisfactory outcome or not (Wedge and Mantle, 1991). Nor is it a simple matter to evaluate outcomes in reconstituted families, where the continuing presence of step-parents and step-children may be differently perceived by each individual family member. It is remarkably difficult to define or identify outcomes for whole families although, given the emphasis upon 'the family' in various aspects of social policy, it is easy for this to be overlooked.

There are, therefore, considerable difficulties in devising an approach to the selection of family outcomes against which the performance of the child care service could be evaluated. It might be most appropriate to monitor behavioural develop-ments, such as changes in parenting skills, or, on the other hand, it may be more helpful to view families as part of a network and examine the strength of different relationships. Family factors may not all have equal significance for every child, so that a 'family outcome' (however defined) may be of considerable evaluative importance for one child but not for another.

Outcomes for Children
The fifth approach to the question 'outcomes for whom?' is to view it from the position of the individual child. What kinds of outcomes are important for the well-being of children? Certain

broad categories have been identified as being of particular significance: for example, the quality of a child's relationships and the extent of his or her networks or the acquisition of practical and academic skills. Each such grouping represents a cluster of more detailed states of affairs which, depending upon the breadth of the focus, could be regarded as significant outcomes for a child.

Such a way of considering outcomes for individual children imposes a professional or at least an adult interpretation of the outcomes that are of special importance. Children's own wishes and desires may be different and reflect the kinds of outcomes that matter to them. Children's immediate wishes should not be disregarded unless these are seen to conflict with their own long-term interests; not only is a child's present sense of well-being an intermediate outcome of value in itself, but it will also have an influence on future development. A happy child is more likely to have the confidence to succeed at school and to develop close relationships with adults and peers than one who is miserable or resentful.

* * *

Thus there is a range of child care outcomes that includes some that are associated with public expectations, some that are a reflection of the corporate nature of social service organizations, others that reflect professional attitudes and beliefs, and yet more that may vary between family members, or from one child to another. Each implies a different way forward in the evaluation of child care. We have chosen to concentrate upon outcomes for individual children. This is neither to ignore the existence of the other kinds of outcomes discussed above nor to suggest that they are less worthy of careful attention. Clearly each is important, not least because none is wholly independent of the others. In the final analysis, however, the child should come first. Indeed, that sentiment is now reflected in the Children Act 1989 which reiterates the rule that paramount consideration should be given to children's welfare in court cases (sect. 1) and lays a new duty on local authorities to safeguard and promote their well-being in all other circumstances (sect. 17).

II Should Greater Weight be Given to Specific or to General Outcomes?

Reference has been made to the conceptual difference between those service outcomes which involve whole categories of children and those which concern individuals. However, there is a further sense in which, even for individual children, distinctions have to be drawn between outcomes that are of a general or composite nature and those that are specific. In considering this issue at least two questions arise:

(i) In how much detail should outcomes in child care be specified?

(ii) How far is the choice of outcomes influenced by ideas about causation?

In How Much Detail Should Outcomes be Specified?

Children are not looked after by local authorities because they are unhappy, but for specific and identifiable reasons. For instance, some of the grounds on which magistrates commit children to care are because they need protection from physical or sexual abuse, because they need to be prevented from harming themselves through drugs, glue-sniffing or alcohol, or because the public needs protection from their anti-social or criminal behaviour. The simplest method of measuring outcomes would be to ask whether the intervention has fulfilled its purpose: is the child protected from further abuse? Has the teenager stopped sniffing glue? Has the young person stopped offending?

Unfortunately, the care services cannot provide a guarantee that specific aims such as these will be met. We know that when children are first looked after by local authorities their behaviour often deteriorates, and those who have not previously offended or harmed themselves may begin to do so (Millham *et al.*, 1978). We also know that public care does not always provide protection from physical, or even sexual, abuse (Levy and Kahan, 1991; Pinkerton and Kelly, 1986; Department of Health and Social Security (Northern Ireland), 1986). Perhaps, therefore, it might be justifiable to restrict the measurement of outcomes to asking whether specific aims such as these have been met. Identifying where local authorities succeed or fail in fulfilling the purposes of an admission would help to improve services, and therefore would benefit the children concerned.

However, to do this would be to measure outcomes solely against public expectations. Although children would benefit, the effect of the interventions on their development would not be the main focus of the exercise; and it is from their perspective that we decided to examine outcomes. For children, a social services intervention can have significant consequences that bear little relationship to its aims. This is particularly true if the intervention is of any duration—and what an adult might see as a short-term intervention may seem quite long from a child's point of view.

Being looked after by a local authority for whatever reason can lead, for instance, to disrupted education, to the weakening of links with relatives and to a poor sense of self-esteem. (Jackson, 1987; Millham *et al.*, 1986; Triseliotis and Russell, 1984). We therefore consider that an adequate means of assessing outcome, while taking account of the specific aims of the original intervention, should also examine the more general question of what effect the local authority's involvement has had on the child's overall potential for achieving long-term well-being. One might object that it is irrelevant to ask whether children who have been committed to care because they steal are, for instance, receiving proper dental treatment: however for the local authority *not* to give proper attention to all aspects of the development of those children it looks after would surely be a dereliction of duty. On the other hand, we would stress that overall aspects of development, which can be fostered without the child needing to be looked after away from home, should not be attended to in place of the main reason for admission: one cannot excuse a failure to prevent a teenager's continued offending on the grounds that he now has beautiful teeth! Thus although a public authority can share its parental respon-sibilities with parents, carers and others, it cannot be selective about which responsibilities are to be undertaken, and which overlooked.

It is more difficult to develop a means of assessing children's general well-being than to examine whether the specific aims of an intervention have been met. Nevertheless, the overall outcome of long-term importance to children can be defined as the achievement of a certain quality of life. If outcomes are defined as generalised conditions then children's lives will be treated as a whole. The various points that need to be considered in devising specific and general indicators of children's quality of life are considered in some detail in the next chapter.

How far is the Choice of Outcomes Influenced by Ideas about Causation?

Professional views about which outcomes are important are influenced by prevailing theories. If, for example, dominant theories link a child's emotional damage to maternal deprivation, then there is likely to be a preoccupation with those outcomes which show that separation from the mother has been prevented or which indicate that satisfactory substitute care has been provided. In this sense outcome is not defined in terms of emotional well-being but rather as the existence of circumstances which are assumed to promote or impair it. Theory serves, therefore, as a means of selecting indicators of well-being or deprivation, and it is these indicators that are frequently taken to be the important outcomes.

These choices are not, however, determined by theoretical presumptions alone, but also by disciplinary orientations. Social workers are likely to concentrate upon family relationships; doctors upon a child's physical condition; teachers upon educational progress and the police upon offending. Each has a somewhat different set of explanations for what causes success or failure in the realm of their concerns. For example, whereas the police pay considerable attention to 'known associates', doctors look for evidence of disease. However, even within different disciplines or services, influential theories (whether explicit or implicit) are liable to change; and that in turn alters what is regarded as a noteworthy outcome.

Most commentators would now subscribe to a multi-factorial explanation of social phenomena. The problem that this raises for those who wish to evaluate child care services is that even the simplest outcome is shaped by some forces that are either unconnected with the service or that lie largely outside its power to control. For purposes of evaluation, therefore, it is tempting to concentrate upon those outcomes that theory and experience suggest are most likely to be susceptible to the influence of service interventions. Indeed, there is a view that, partly because of the application of the 'rule of optimism' (Dingwall *et al.*, 1983), expectations of what can be achieved by social workers in modifying behaviour or improving relationships are set unrealistically high, with the result that the outcomes that are offered for evaluation inevitably show their achievements to have fallen short in one way or another. There is a pressing need to focus upon outcomes that are not over-ambitious and which take account of the range and strength of the non-social work factors that affect what happens—or what does not happen. However, this should not be allowed to justify the selection of outcomes that reflect poor standards of service or unreasonably low expectations.

These matters raise the issue of outcomes as goals. Planning in child care entails the determination of objectives which, once specified, tend to become the subjects of evaluation. Meeting, or failing to meet a goal becomes tantamount to evaluation, whether it be a service goal or a goal in work with particular children and families. Yet so much turns upon the kinds of goals that it is fashionable to set (and over what period). This is influenced by training and, as we have said, by the theories that underpin that training, as well as by political priorities and prevailing styles of management. For instance, a hundred years ago, signing the pledge against alcohol was considered an important outcome for children brought up in the voluntary societies. In short, outcomes are not free-standing states of affairs waiting to be discovered and then evaluated; they are the products of an often complicated process of selection that is shaped by the interplay of different interests, different assumptions and different aspirations.

III   When are Outcomes Considered to Occur?

An 'outcome' implies a conclusion. Yet in reality events are progressive, interactive and, short of death, rarely final. Hence, the question of when something has become an outcome is of considerable importance. It is likely to vary between people according to both their personal perspective and their general attitude towards time. This is especially important in considering child care outcomes from the viewpoint of the children concerned.

The outcomes that matter to children are likely to be more immediate than those that concern adults. Likewise, deprived children and their families are unlikely to think in terms of long-term outcomes. Social workers, too, tend to focus on intermediate outcomes connected with the short-term objectives that are created by specialization, by administrative and legal requirements, and by the problem of dealing with a succession of crises. For example, the very fact that children cease to be looked after by local authorities after they reach adulthood imposes a certain constraint upon the way that outcomes are conceived. Yet long-term outcomes may be more important, and they may prove to be quite different from those of a more intermediate nature (see, for example, Quinton and Rutter, 1988).

Evaluations will be affected as time perspectives change. The whole issue of when an outcome becomes identified as such, and an evaluation of it made, is of central importance to the role of research in child care. The time available for a study has to dictate which outcomes are selected for scrutiny: they have to be phenomena that occur (or fail to occur) within the lifetime of a project.

Thus time crucially influences how outcomes are viewed. In particular, three time-related issues should be considered:
   (i)   The sequential nature of outcomes
   (ii)   The time periods that are especially appropriate for children
   (iii) Routine outcomes

The Sequential Nature of Outcomes

The notion of sequential outcomes should occupy a more prominent place in thinking about child care evaluation. Such a formulation would accommodate the idea of intermediate outcomes; but it would also be compatible with the step-by-step approach that is often the reality of social work practice. Indeed, a linked sequence of outcomes representing stages towards some more general and long-term goal would certainly fit into the current emphasis in the new Children Act upon planning, monitoring, review and, if necessary, revision.

Professional and administrative practice, as well as the law, focus upon identifiable events or episodes. The structures that they provide for the child care service are formed of beginnings and endings. Typically, the impetus for action arises because something new has happened which calls for a response: a young child has been found alone at night; a court makes a care order; a child runs away from a residential home; a mother brings her teenage daughter to a social services office declaring that she will not have her in the house a moment longer. From a social worker's point of view events such as these will be seen as the start of an episode. Yet for many of the other participants they will be seen as outcomes or culminations. Crises rarely occur without a discernible history that includes a sequence of previous outcomes. Likewise, just as the new episode is the outcome of something else, so the outcomes upon which child care tends to focus are yet other beginnings. Arrivals become departures.

The distinction between 'being in care' and 'not being in care' has for too long been a defining characteristic of the child care service; the attempt made in the Children Act 1989 to blur this boundary suggests that the processes described above have finally begun to be recognised. The idea of children's 'care careers' has also taken root, with the notion of the child at risk becoming well established as well (see, for example, Millham et al., 1986). Nevertheless, the public face of child care remains an amalgam of officially defined episodes. This is likely to distort the way in which outcomes are evaluated. For example, the admission of a child to 'care' has often been regarded as an undesirable step, in many cases signalling the 'failure' of previous efforts to prevent such an occurrence. Yet, as the Children Act 1989 recognises, for a local authority to provide accommodation or care may offer new opportunities or enable everyone to take stock as a crisis abates.

Unless outcomes are viewed as sequences (that is, as chains of events) it is tempting to evaluate them in isolation. Looked at against what went before and compared with what follows next an 'outcome' may seem neither as bad nor as good as it did when regarded as a solitary episode.

Appropriate Time Periods for Children

One cannot know with certainty what 'outcomes' mean for children. What are the events that matter to them? Being looked after by a local authority, having to appear in court or experiencing their parents' divorce are significant events for most children. Yet, especially for younger children, it is the interpersonal processes that these events symbolise that matter most. This has implications for the way in which the selection of outcomes in child care is approached. Not only is it necessary to focus upon intermediate rather than final outcomes but also upon what might be called micro-outcomes which, at a certain point, become indistinguishable from children's experience of daily interactions.

Although children certainly have fears and hopes about the future (indeed children's feelings of security or insecurity depend a good deal upon what they expect to happen) their sense of well-being is not only a reflection of their experience of micro-events but also of their experience over relatively short periods. This needs to be taken seriously, not least because children's present welfare can so easily be overlooked in an adult preoccuption with safeguarding their future. The quality of life of younger children is heavily dependent upon how they are cared for day by day. A concern with more distant outcomes should not be allowed to obscure that fact. After all, it is precisely the quality of these intimate and daily experiences that are widely assumed to shape the longer-term outcomes.

However, there is a dilemma because those who assume a parental role need to exercise precautionary and promotional foresight on behalf of the children for whom they are responsible. Parents need to set objectives, take action and check on outcomes. Good parents do not allow a child's preferences to prevail if they consider them to be prejudicial to some future state of well-being. Even so, few parents follow a detailed blueprint which leads towards the realization of some grandly-conceived objective or outcome for their children. In most cases things are more ordinary than that, and although most parents' time perspectives are longer than those of their children, they too remain relatively short—not necessarily in terms of aspirations but certainly in terms of action. They take one thing at a time: they worry about health today, education tomorrow and friendships the next day. They are guided in what they do by a series of comparatively short-term concerns with detail—albeit that these concerns reflect a general wish to do the best they can for their children.

Yet there are occasions when parents recognise, and are called upon to make or to be involved in, strategic decisions about their children. These decisions, about such matters as where and with whom a child should live after divorce, or moving to another part of the country away from extended family, established friends and familiar schooling, have their parallels in the child care service, particularly when there is a need to place a child in a permanent alternative family. These are issues that call for longer time perspectives, both in considering what the outcomes might be and in examining what they actually are.

Hence, there is a balance to be achieved in child care between short and long-term objectives and therefore between shorter and longer-term outcomes. Any scheme of evaluation that concentrates exclusively upon the one rather than the other is unikely to ensure that children's best interests are promoted as successfully as possible.

Routine Outcomes
The outcomes that capture attention are often associated with critical events. If these are used as bases for evaluation then the

results may unduly reflect what is dramatic or extraordinary. For that reason, as has already been suggested, there is much to be said for fixing points, such as the six-monthly reviews of children looked after by local authorities, in order to monitor and record what has been happening. The advantages of such procedures are: first, that they do not necessarily assume that only notable events should be treated as outcomes; secondly, that they are not conducted in response to a crisis (with all its distorting influences); and, finally, that they offer an opportunity to consider how much progress has been made towards a desired outcome rather than only whether or not an objective has been realised.

IV   Outcomes and Evaluation

A major object of our deliberations was to conceptualise and identify a range of outcomes in child care which could be used as a basis for evaluating the progress of individual children and therefore, by extension, the performance of the child care services. In moving from outcomes to their evaluation however, we were obliged to face the question of what values were to be ascribed to particular results. Obviously, the choice of something as an outcome is shaped by a belief that it distinguishes between (or helps to distinguish between) a good or bad situation for a child. Certain outcomes are considered to be more important than others because they are, or are associated with, conditions which are thought to be desirable or (as negative indicators) undesirable.

However carefully they are chosen most outcomes cannot simply be classified as 'successes' or 'failures'. There are usually gradations, and failure in one area may be offset by success in another. These issues raise problems of scaling and combination: how do we establish *partial* success, and can we balance outcomes in one sphere (or along one dimension) against outcomes in another in order to arrive at some overall assessment? How, for example, do we determine that there has been a *moderate* amount of success in improving a child's health; and how, then, do we set that against, say, loss of family contacts but improvements in his or her standard of education?

Over and above these questions stands the problem of relativity. Partial success in this or that area for one child may be an outstanding achievement for another, depending upon their relative starting positions, their different handicaps or inherent capabilities. One only has to think what nonsense it would be to apply the same interpretation of certain outcomes to a child with severe learning problems as to one who faces no such challenge. Even so, much turns upon what is considered to be attainable, and certainly there are many examples of the way in which expectations have changed over the years. However, our demands of the child care services may still be too low, not only because of the nature of their history but also because they have been mainly concerned with a small group of children and families who suffer from an oppressive assortment of deprivations, disadvantages and disruptions. In short, the range and intensity of their problems make it difficult to evaluate outcomes in ways which would be appropriate for those who do not suffer such handicaps.

That does not mean, however, that the significant dimensions of outcomes in child care need to be, or should be, different from those that would be generally applicable; but what has to be carefully considered, and sometimes adjusted, is the evaluative interpretation placed upon attainments. The importance of this will be apparent in succeeding chapters and especially when we explain and describe the evaluative instrument that we have devised. That instrument has been constructed around seven areas (or dimensions) of children's development: their health; their education; their social relationships; their competence in everyday situations; their sense of identity; their emotional and behavioral development, and their social presentation. The rationale for this selection is discussed in chapter 6, as are the components of each of the clusters. Obviously, these seven dimensions of development are relevant for any child. However, as we have been at pains to emphasise, that does not mean that how one child's position in any of these areas is *evaluated* will be the same as the evaluation for another. It all depends upon where they start and what is expected.

Nevertheless, norms are important. Even though we take children's backgrounds into account in deciding how their present circumstances are to be assessed it is still necessary to be aware of the extent to which those circumstances or achievements deviate from generally prevailing norms.

Deciding on perspectives and time-scales, choosing which outcomes are significant and when, and identifying norms against which 'scores' can be evaluated, all serve to clarify the task. However, the selection of tools which produce both valid and reliable assessments demands further complex choices. Chapter 3 considers some of the more technical and theoretical issues that arise in the process of evaluation, and chapter 4 examines how the outcomes that have been identified and measured are to be *explained*.

Summary of the Main Points from this Chapter

1. The choice of outcomes to measure, and the interpretation of the results, will vary according to the perspectives from which they are viewed. Five different types of outcome are important in child care: public outcomes, service outcomes, professional outcomes, family outcomes and child outcomes. Because the central aim of the child care service should be to ensure the welfare of children in need, we have chosen to concentrate on measuring outcomes for individual children.

2. An apparently simple method of evaluating outcomes might be to examine how far the specific aims of the intervention are being met. However, to do so would be to ignore the other more general consequences of the intervention on the child's long-term well-being. The most useful means of evaluating outcome would seek to assess how a local authority fulfils *all* rather than *some* of its parental responsibilities.

3. Our choice of which outcomes to measure will be influenced by the professional orientation of those who make the selection, by cultural factors and by the assumptions and aims we hold for the children to be assessed.

4. An adequate system of assessment must take into account the sequential nature of outcomes, the child's own time perspective, and the need to examine progress on a routine basis.

5. Unless assessments are based on norms that are prevalent in the general population it will not be possible to identify those areas in which disadvantaged children fall behind their peers. However, the method of evaluation must be sufficiently flexible to take account of special factors such as physical or mental handicap which will alter the weight given to an individual child's achievements. Results should indicate where strengths in one area offset weaknesses in another.

Chapter 3

Principles of Measurement and Evaluation

So far, we have attempted to define and analyse the concept of outcome and discussed some of the problems that arise from differences in perspective, priorities, timescale, theoretical orientation and values. Here, we take a step back to consider more generally the principles of outcome evaluation, for it is only with reference to these that the adequacy of any proposed scheme or approach can itself be judged. The revision and improvement of evaluative instruments should be a continuing matter for concern, and that calls for yardsticks against which their performance can be assessed.

The ideal measure of outcome is both dynamic and relative: dynamic in the sense that it assesses changes over time and relative in that it compares those changes either with what would have happened in some other circumstances or with some norm or other 'external' point of reference. However, as we indicated in the last chapter, measurement, assessment and evaluation are all closely interrelated, and the choice of a particular approach is not only influenced by the desire to achieve validity and reliability; it also depends on the reasons why the assessment is being undertaken.

I   Styles of Assessment and Evaluation

In designing any scheme of outcome and evaluation a number of basic decisions have to be made, although none of them is mutually exclusive.

(i)   To what extent is the assessment intended to run in parallel with day-to-day practice?

(ii) Is the objective to obtain cross-sectional or longitudinal data?

(iii) Is the information obtained to be quantitative or qualitative?

(iv) Is the system of assessment to be comprehensive or indicative?

Some of these questions have already been touched on, but in what follows we consider more closely the issues involved and the reasons for making particular choices in relation to the assessment of outcomes for children looked after or supervised by local authorities.

How far is Evaluation to be Integrated with Practice?

Although virtually all evaluation in child care has been intended to influence policy or practice, or both, the ways in which it has been approached have varied. Two distinct types can be identified. On the one hand there is a style of evaluation which aims to feed back its results into policy or practice only after enough time has elapsed to have built up a picture of what has happened. It tends to be fixed term, focussed on particular questions and concerned with the generalisations that can be derived from aggregated results. On the other hand there is another type of evaluation that is designed as part of a continuing process in which information is made available regularly to participants in a way that is intended to influence their behaviour directly.

These two approaches, which are often termed 'summative' and 'formative' in the American literature, are each vigorously advocated by their respective adherents. However, this should not obscure the fact that in practice there can be a good deal of overlap and mixture. Nevertheless, the differences between the two approaches are significant and it is plainly important for those designing schemes of evaluation to decide, in principle, which they favour. Different circumstances, different interests and different objectives will dictate where the emphasis is to lie.

The criticisms of the first, or 'summative' approach (Parlett and Hamilton, 1976; Patton, 1978) are that its results are too far removed from the original events to have anything but a long-delayed impact on practice or policy. Furthermore, the results tend to be presented in final (and formal) reports to managers and policy-makers, often by-passing the practitioners and those with whom they work.

By contrast, the second style of evaluation (the 'formative', so-called) is deliberately designed to provide running results that assist those involved to achieve their objectives. Of course, this approach also has its critics who, for example, warn of the risk of the evaluations being 'contaminated' by the constant modification that it aims to secure. They also point out the difficulty in obtaining a clear view of how a system is working overall and therefore of what adjustments in, for instance, resource allocations should be made.

We did not consider that either set of criticisms gave conclusive grounds for rejecting one or other of the approaches that we have outlined. However, we did decide that any evaluative instrument which we proposed should offer social workers and care-givers as much direct and current information about processes and outcomes as possible. Likewise, we were concerned that wherever feasible children and parents should also be involved in the evaluations. Thus, in developing a scheme for assessing outcomes we were drawn towards the second or 'formative' model of evaluation.

The Value of Longitudinal Data
The difficulty of identifying causal processes in the care and development of children is a theme that runs right through this book. Clearly most outcomes are determined by many factors, only some of which will be related to the care provided by the local authority. Nevertheless, if the study of child care outcomes is to have any effect on practice we have to assume that the activities of social workers and carers are not neutral and that connections can be made between what they do (or do not do) and what happens to the children for whom they are responsible.

Quinton and Rutter (1988) have shown that early risk experiences, which will be common in the lives of most children in contact with social services, are intensified by later adverse circumstances but that they can also be ameliorated by later beneficial experiences. A negative outcome may only occur if the individual encounters a particular situation that activates the vulnerability produced by the risk factor; for example, homelessness or having to live in make-shift accommodation used by other vulnerable people. There are also turning points in people's lives, such as a major illness or a new relationship, that serve to intensify or reduce the risk factors. However, these intervening events are often obscured in cross-sectional studies that use one-off assessments. One of the most important advantages of longitudinal data is that they provide the opportunity to investigate changes in the individual as well as the way in which different individuals are differently affected by similar changes.

From a practice viewpoint the arguments for a longitudinal approach to outcome evaluation are self-evident. By providing comparable information over time the social worker is enabled to take an overview of a child's care career, to see what has been achieved and what needs to be done, to build on successes and take remedial action where necessary. On the research side, longitudinal strategies have many advantages which have been set out by Rutter (1988). These include: the ability to be precise about the timing, measurement and sequence of experiences (retrospective studies suffer from the unreliability of subjects' memories on these points); the possibility of studying the process by which a particular risk variable may lead to several different maladaptive outcomes, and the analysis of what he calls 'direct causal chain mechanisms'. Such mechanisms were well illustrated by Quinton and Rutter's (1988) follow-up study of girls brought up in a children's home. The major protective influence which enabled them to provide good parenting for their own children was the presence in adult life of support from a non-deviant spouse. However, having such a partner was not just a matter of good luck. It was influenced by the social settings in which the young women found themselves and particularly by whether or not, in late adolescence, they had shown a tendency to plan ahead. This, in its turn, depended on their having had positive experiences at school. Thus, the 'outcome' was not decided by any single event—'both risk and protective mechanisms derived from a chain of continuities and discontinuities over time that served to increase or decrease the likelihood of a maladaptive outcome' (Quinton and Rutter, 1988; p.20). Chain effects of this kind can only be discerned by having comparable data on individuals over long periods of time.

Although Rutter's emphasis is mainly on the opportunities which longitudinal data provide for tracing causal connections between adverse experiences and subsequent pathology, he does also point to the fact that one major advantage of longitudinal data is the opportunity that they offer to study 'escape from risk'. What is it, for example, that enables some individuals who have suffered very adverse childhood experiences to become competent adults and good parents to their own children? Identifying the protective factors could provide valuable leads to child care workers wondering where to focus their efforts.

For reasons such as these we decided to adopt a longitudinal approach. Apart from its intrinsic advantages, such an approach is implicit in the choice of a 'formative' model of evaluation. However, these decisions raised practical questions about the timing and frequency of assessment. We leave these for the moment but return to them later in the chapter.

Quantitative and Qualitative Methods: The Problems of Scaling
There has been a long-running tension between quantitative and qualitative approaches in social research which has been reflected clearly in the field of policy and practice evaluation (Finch, 1988). Quantitative methods are often seen as objective and rigorous as against qualitative methods which, by contrast, tend to be regarded as soft, subjective and speculative. Of course, much turns on the care and thoroughness with which each method is used and, in practice, they are often combined in

evaluative research. Nonetheless, there remain issues about the primary orientation of such work and about the balance of approaches. These have to be addressed. One of the central questions concerns the scaling of outcomes along the chosen dimensions.

All too often in the social sciences the development of scales proceeds in ignorance of the basic requirements concerning the level and type of measurement needed or attainable in a particular context (Knapp, 1989). There is a danger that measuring instruments which seek to reduce complicated phenomena to a statistical form will acquire an appearance of objectivity and certainty which is in fact spurious. Although the technical aspects of scale construction are too complex to consider in any detail here (see, for example, Stevens, 1946), it became evident to us that there were formidable methodological obstacles to the development of scales which would have the required qualities of validity, reliability, sensitivity and manageability with respect to most of our seven dimensions.

A more fundamental objection to such an exercise is that most scales are abstractions which have meaning only when the results of applying them are aggregated and interpreted. They would have limited value unless validated on suitable populations (an enormous task). As applied to individuals they also carry the risk of encouraging labelling and reinforcing low expectations. Moreover, although they may indicate to carers or social workers that there is cause for concern they do not usually give any clue as to how matters might be improved.

A further difficulty is that such measures usually need to be administered by people with specialist knowledge. Although social workers could be trained to use them, they would not see it as part of their normal work. Scales designed to produce quantifiable results would be unlikely to meet the criterion of being manageable enough to be used by social workers in conjunction with those providing primary care, and in some cases, with the children themselves.

In the light of these considerations it was decided to adopt an approach to the construction of a measuring instrument for which we are not aware of any precedents. This is described in detail in chapter 7, but essentially it entailed the specification of a number of desired outcomes or aims that were related to the age of the child in each dimension of well-being and asking social workers to indicate (on an uncalibrated scale) how far these had been achieved at the time of the assessment. Although this is a 'soft' measure to the extent that it relies on the subjective judgement of the person completing the assessment record, it can be quantified by assigning numerical values to positions on the scale.

The substance of the assessment, however, is sandwiched between the aims and the outcome judgements, growing from the one and contributing to the other. As will be explained more fully in chapter 7, each of the aims is associated with the conditions that will make it more likely that the desired outcomes will occur. These are cast in the form of questions to social workers and care-givers (or to the children themselves) which point to necessary actions and provide the basis for the judgement of outcomes. They thus fulfil the requirement of giving immediate feedback to practitioners and can, as we propose in chapter 8, be built into their normal work while also providing a rich bank of factual and qualitative data, albeit that not all of it will be strictly comparable as between children. Nonetheless, such a bank will provide a valuable basis for a variety of further research.

Comprehensive or Indicative Measures
Although, for the reasons explained above, it was decided that the attempt to develop a comprehensive array of outcome measures would be unproductive, that did not necessarily rule out the use of a different kind of assessment scale which would not aim to specify outcomes in detail but rather use a number of indicators in order to obtain an overall measure of a child's well-being. An example of such a scale which has been extremely useful to researchers is Rutter's Malaise Inventory. This asks for a yes or no response to a series of questions about symptoms, producing a final score which can then be related to other factors in a person's life.

Other instruments which aim to measure general conditions employ positive or combinations of positive and negative indicators. Whatever their precise construction the assumption is that indicators of various dimensions of the quality of life can be scored and then added together to give an aggregate that locates an individual somewhere on a scale or gradient. Higher scores on one dimension may compensate for lower scores on another. This has the drawback that a person's overall position on the continuum may remain unchanged even if the component elements of a score are thoroughly reshuffled, making it of rather limited use in longitudinal studies or for the tracing of causal connections.

One way of combining results obtained from assessing different dimensions into a single outcome measure is to place relative valuations on combinations of characteristics, and this technique has been employed to interesting effect in health care contexts; for example, in the quality-adjusted-life-year (QALY) measures developed by Rosser (1983) and Torrance (1986). An important feature of their work is that trade-offs between dimensions are made explicit, and are based on applied research aimed at teasing out the views of a group of experts, a sample of service professionals and actual or potential service-users. This is much to be preferred to the *ad hoc* summation of scores on different outcome items which is commonly (and unapologetically) to be found in some of the child care literature.

However, it is by no means widely accepted that the conflation of scores on different dimensions into a one-dimensional scale is either feasible or sensible. We took the view that at this stage it was better to take forward a *set* of outcome dimensions and a *set* of associated measures than to force them into a single straitjacket. This has the advantage of offering a degree of flexibility in policy and practice; it also avoids attaching a weight, indicating their relative importance, to different dimensions, a procedure which is as value-laden as any other stage of outcome measurement and is liable to give the misleading appearance of scientific objectivity.

On the other hand it could be argued that weighting simply makes explicit and open an unavoidable process that goes on all the time. Of course, the different dimensions of child welfare are not independent of each other, and one of the important purposes of looking at possible procedures for their integration is to ensure that this interdependence is acknowledged in the outcome measurement process. However, the use of an overall outcome measure derived from indicators might have the effect of obscuring the relationships rather than illuminating them, and it would certainly not help in the recognition of causal chain effects. Furthermore, outcome measures that do not conflate different dimensions have the advantage that the data can be combined in different ways by different people according to their own needs and priorities.

Certainly, social work practice assumes the existence of a hierarchy of needs, for this is how care and placement decisions are made. Social workers are continually obliged to trade off possible and actual achievements, paying greater attention to one factor at the expense of others. At some stage *somebody* has to make decisions about the relative importance of different dimensions. If this is done within the outcomes assessment process it has the advantage of being explicit, but it also acquires a fixity which may be unhelpful. At the case level the hierarchy of dimensions may depend on the circumstances of a particular child at a specific time. For example, in the term before a young person is due to sit a public examination, continuity of schooling might be the top priority. At another time promoting contact with the young person's natural family might take precedence. Likewise, at the policy level priorities and perceptions shift in line with changes in political control and pressure on resources as well as the inter-play of ideas and evolving experience.

For all these reasons it was decided not to build any weighting of dimensions into the assessment scheme nor, at this stage, to attempt to collapse them into a one-dimensional measure of children's well-being. That does not necessarily rule out such an exercise in the future. Indeed, if such a method of assessing child care outcomes could be developed it might be extremely useful, especially to researchers and managers. However, a great deal more research would need to be done first to provide a reliable basis for the selection of relevant indicators, and major scientific hurdles remain to be cleared.

II   The Time Dimension

The adoption of a longitudinal approach means that outcomes need to be measured as changes in circumstances and characteristics over time. The continuous monitoring of well-being would be theoretically ideal but impossible in practice; we need therefore to find the best compromise. To that end three practical questions have to be answered as well as two others of a more theoretical nature. They are:

(i)   What is the most appropriate start date for the assessment of child welfare?

(ii)   What is the most appropriate end date?

(iii) How frequently between these two dates do we need to make assessments?

(iv)   How can we weigh the known outcomes of the present against the, as yet, unrealised and uncertain outcomes of the future?

(v)   Should adjustments be made to the criteria for evaluation over time in order to reflect shifting values and expectations in society?

In order fully to evaluate the impact of 'care' on the development of an individual child he or she would need to be assessed on standardised tests or scales well before entering the system. Just before, or soon after admission can only be second best benchmarks, since the child's welfare is likely to be affected already by the emotional upheaval that usually precedes and accompanies relocation.

When children come into 'care' at a time of crisis very little may have been known about them prior to admission. In a large-scale study in Suffolk of social work decision-making in relation to a cohort of children entering care, attempts were made, from information obtained from social workers at a later date, to build a baseline data set describing a child's circumstances and welfare before admission. Not surprisingly, there were wide differences in the amount of information available at this stage. Some children had been well-known to the social workers for a long time before admission, others had not (Knapp, Bryson and Lewis, 1985). Particular difficulty will follow when events and circumstances change quickly, as is common around the time of entry into 'care' (Aldgate, 1977; Millham *et al.*, 1986). Ideally, then, our outcome measurement should start from the date of a child's contact with a care agency, or as soon as it becomes evident that a significant degree of intervention will be necessary. In practice the point of entry into care (or accommodation) may be a more realistic time for a full assessment.

Choosing an end date for the period of assessment is even more problematic. The ideal would be to study the child over his or her full life-span on the reasonable assumption that differential childhood experiences have an impact upon subsequent life experiences. This is impractical, but if enough resources were available it would be desirable to assess a child's circumstances at some time—say one year—after the end of a care period or after the cessation of any post-discharge service that departments might be providing. Under the Children Act 1989, these services may be extended up to the age of twenty-one.

Choosing the length of the follow-up period is not easy. Work on juvenile crime suggests that a high proportion of offenders stop (or, perhaps, stop getting caught) once they acquire family and employment responsibilities. Thus, a follow-up study of offending which conducted its assessment too far into adulthood would be likely to miss any shorter-term differential impact of alternative custodial and non-custodial placements. Many high risk adolescents, viewed ten years later, present less distressing problems than one might have predicted from the perspective of their late teens. On the other hand, too short a follow-up period may be insufficient to allow the full effects of alternative interventions to work themselves through, or may give the wrong impression. When Triseliotis (1980a, 1984) retrospectively assessed educational achievements at age sixteen, he found that the standard of those in residential care had been higher than that of children who had been fostered. The difference was apparently related to the higher aspirations of residential care staff. However, a later assessment revealed that the children from residential settings had lost their comparative advantage after discharge, when other long-term benefits of foster care came into play.

The timing of assessments will also be influenced by whether the object is to assess the impact of a child being looked after away from home or of other social work intervention; in the first case the timing would be related to 'care' episodes, in the second it would occur at regular intervals throughout and after the period of contact.

In general there has been a tendency for evaluation to focus on longer-term care, and for short-term admissions and placements to be ignored or to be assessed only on their effectiveness in solving specific problems. However, about a third of the children who come into 'care' for a brief period will be readmitted at a later date and many short admissions are in reality episodes in intermittent long-term care. Even when a short-term admission is an isolated event it can still form part of a 'causal chain mechanism' (Rutter, 1988) which can be either beneficial or damaging to the child's overall development.

For instance, a short period away from home in local authority 'care' may be but one of many other disruptions that a child has suffered quite outside the realm of the social work services. It is certainly difficult to assess the part that short-term service interventions play in improving or safeguarding a child's welfare, but the adoption of a longitudinal perspective in evaluation will reduce the difficulty.

Since it is not practicable to evaluate child care by any form of continous monitoring, it is necessary to choose a number of intermediate assessment dates. Whatever the choice, these dates will be used as points of reference in order to estimate the character of changes over time. A simple before and after design, with only start and end date assessments, assumes a smooth progression (upwards or downwards) from one point to the other, whereas with assessments repeated at regular intervals we have the possibility of indentifying any fluctuations in the welfare of children as the care episode develops and relating these to social work interventions. In chapter 7 we propose that full assessments should occur at least annually and interim assessments not less than six-monthly, in line with the statutory review system.

A problem that arises in the evaluation of outcomes is that, as we have pointed out in the previous chapter, future or later levels of welfare are less important to most people (and especially to children) than present or immediate experience. We value a particular level of welfare today more highly than the same or even a superior level of welfare at some future date. This being so, any long-term evaluation of outcomes will need to incorporate some means of balancing present against future states of well-being. Here is not the place to discuss the host of conceptual issues such matters raise; nevertheless, it is important to indicate that there are problems in interpreting welfare changes observed over long time-spans.

Further difficulties are created by the way in which emphases shift over longish periods of time; for example, the criteria for successful intervention may alter; contextual factors which impinge upon achievements may change; different preferences, or new theories and ideas may challenge old-established assumptions. Similarly, different issues assume importance as children grow up and move into new social settings, such as school and work. It is unlikely therefore that any single assessment instrument could be appropriate across the whole age range. We have recognised this by designing separate schedules for different age groups, with more at the younger end when the most rapid development occurs.

A second aspect of the way in which emphases shift over time might be called the 'climatic' effect—changes both in social conditions and in attitudes. Consider, for instance, how in the Newson and Newson (1968) study of children growing up in Nottingham, many of the four year-olds were expected to run errands to the local shop, a task no longer generally considered acceptable, necessary or safe. West's (1967) follow-up study of delinquency began by looking for traits at age eight that would predict offending at age fourteen. In the meantime, however, the new 'interactionist criminology' arrived and took hold, so that by the time the results were published the ideas looked dated and were criticised; the methodology had not permitted adaptation to new theories. More recently, however, West's work has been reviewed more favourably, reminding us that there are swings of the pendulum. Other examples may emerge in the future; for instance, in a time of mass unemployment, being out of work in adolescence can no longer be regarded as a sign of social pathology, whilst AIDS has come to redefine the significance of sexual behaviour. Some issues that were previously rarely if ever raised, such as ritual child abuse, have become prominent.

Changes in the climate of ideas and assumptions may be difficult to detect on a day-to-day level. Their very slowness may make it unlikely that they will be identified as significant until well after the ideas that they supplant have ceased to be generally accepted. That possibility always needs to be borne in mind.

III   Making Comparisons

For both practice and research purposes a means of making comparisons is essential. The significance of outcomes can only be evaluated by reference to some kind of comparative standard. The basic principles of outcome measurement could be most reliably applied in practice if we were able to determine a child's level of well-being following the provision of a care service and then turn the clock back and examine the impact of a different type of intervention or no intervention at all. Obviously, this is impossible. It is necessary, therefore, to select a suitable strategy that approximates to the ideal. A common and useful classification of such 'approximating' devices distinguishes between comparative designs and single group designs. The difference between them is that the former include separate control or comparison groups whereas the lattter focus only on the individuals receiving a service. Let us explain in a little more detail the strengths and weaknesses of each approach.

The comparative design is firmly located in the tradition of scientific research. It has the advantage of not relying on any externally imposed norm or judgement which may have little relevance for some cultural or ethnic groups, for certain areas of the country, or for particular periods. Nevertheless, comparative designs harbour their own problems; for example, the difficulty of achieving a close match of any 'control' and 'experimental' groups, and in the randomised allocation of services there are the ethical problems of deliberately withholding a service from half the people being studied. That, as some commentators have argued (Rossi and Freeman, 1982), could lead to 'arbitrarily and capriciously depriving control groups of positive benefits'. Opposition to randomisation is also prompted by the feeling that vulnerable people are the unknowing subjects of some 'experiment'. The fact that every policy change is to some extent 'experimental' goes unrecognised. Rutter and Giller (1983) argue in relation to juvenile delinquency, for example, that experimental interventions that are evaluated are not only entirely ethical but essential.

Whatever the strength of the ethical objections to certain types of comparative design may be, there still remain considerable practical problems. Take, for example, quasi-experiments which attempt to identify and select control groups comparable in important respects with the experimental group by a process of 'matching'. The aim of matching would be to pair off children in the experimental and control groups who, if given identical care, would be expected to have identical outcomes. Pairing individuals in this way is not easy and demands a familiarity with the underlying processes that link interventions with outcomes, a familiarity which will not be available, by definition, in many of the circumstances in which evaluation is needed.

Taking these other factors into consideration we decided that the most appropriate way forward in devising an evaluative instrument would be to adopt a 'single group' design. Of course, as we have seen, such a design can incorporate controls of a kind. They can be the same group before intervention ('reflexive' controls); an established norm or norms ('generic' controls), or some judgement or expectation formed by expert opinion or a cross-section of a 'relevant' public ('shadow' controls).

The approach that we adopted incorporated both 'generic' and 'shadow' controls. The generic control was derived from the idea of what 'reasonable' parents would consider a good outcome for their own children, which, in its turn, was derived from the philosophy of the Children Act 1989. The shadow controls derived from research findings and professional judgements. The implied comparison group is, therefore, children growing up in their own 'average' families who are neither especially advantaged nor disadvantaged.

Although the choice of a single group design appears to rule out an 'experimental' approach to the evaluation of outcomes, in the longer-term it may well facilitate what might be termed 'natural experiments'. For example, the outcome measures associated with our seven dimensions will lend themselves to aggregation in various ways and thereby could help to establish the overall standard of practice within a social services team, a particular setting, or a local authority. Furthermore, the fact that the measures are based on general population norms means that they are suitable for use later in comparative designs. On the other hand the qualitative material they contain should also make them a rich source of insights for practitioners and help to generate future research questions.

As we have indicated in this chapter, the assessment and evaluation of outcomes is fraught with methodological problems, and we cannot claim to have overcome them all. The Assessment and Action Record that is described in chapter 7 is a step towards the development of a satisfactory instrument for assessing outcomes in child care, which we hope will be further refined and developed as it is increasingly used. By relating the practical decisions we were obliged to make in constructing the instrument to more theoretical issues in outcome evaluation we have tried to indicate fruitful directions for further work.

Summary of the Main Points from this Chapter

1. This chapter reviews some of the theoretical considerations which had to be taken into account in the construction of the assessment and monitoring instrument described in chapter 7. The advantages and difficulties associated with different types of measurement are discussed in the context of child care.

2. The need for the system of assessment to be accessible and useful to practitioners points to an approach in which the information obtained can be used directly by social workers and care-givers as a basis for action. This is contrasted with an alternative approach to evaluation, in which the outcome is measured at an end point and any impact on practice is filtered through researchers and managers.

3. Forms of assessment may be designed to obtain cross-sectional or longitudinal data. The advantages of longitudinal data in research on child welfare have been clearly demonstrated, making it possible to investigate changes in an individual over time as well as between individuals and groups. Tracing causal processes, which usually involve complex chains of continuities and discontinuities, depends on the availability of reliable information for the same subject over an extended period of time. This suggests that the assessment of outcomes should be cumulative and designed to be repeated at regular intervals. Not only can such a scheme provide an invaluable body of data for researchers, it also helps social workers to develop an overview of a child's care career and to distinguish between temporary fluctuations and long-term trends.

4. Attempting to measure and evaluate outcomes poses many questions; for instance, whether the approach should be quantitative or qualitative and in what form the data obtained should be expressed. The use of scales as measuring instruments was found to have methodological weaknesses and a limited potential

for influencing practice. The scheme that the working party proposes is a mixture of the two approaches, incorporating factual information, observation and professional judgements, but allowing for differences of opinion and descriptive material to be noted. The data are recorded in such a way as to be easily quantifiable for research purposes but remain accessible to care-givers and social workers.

5. Linked to the previous issue is the question whether the aim is to produce an overall measure of child well-being or indicative assessments of development along a number of different dimensions. The reasons for choosing the second option are explained.

6. The decision to adopt a longitudinal approach highlights the importance of the time dimension, raising practical questions of start and end dates and the frequency of assessment as well as problems such as the relative weighting given to short and longer-term outcomes and the impact of shifting values and expectations.

7. Moving from individual case evaluation to group comparisons raises further dilemmas. Although experimental designs, in which, for example, children are randomly allocated to different forms of treatment, are theoretically possible, they pose difficult ethical and practical issues. However, the use of a standard assessment instrument with large numbers of children in the course of ordinary practice opens up the possibility of 'natural experiments' which could produce important new insights into the immediate and future consequences of different types of intervention.

8. The proposed assessment scheme represents a compromise between what might be scientifically desirable and what is practically feasible and useful to the people concerned. It is a first step towards assessing outcomes rather than a final answer.

Chapter 4

Relating Outcomes to Interventions

As we have explained, neither the identification of an outcome nor its measurement is a simple matter. Yet even when a satisfactory solution to these problems has been found, a further important question remains to be addressed. How are we to explain the outcomes that have been established? Of course, improvements in, say, a child's sense of identity or in the quality of his or her attachments are desirable changes in their own right. However, it is difficult to be sure how far such achievements are attributable to the intervention of social work or other services. Without further theoretical analysis therefore, it is doubtful how far the evaluation of outcomes can be used as a reliable guide to the effect and quality of such interventions since changes (for better or for worse) may be the result of factors that operate well beyond the province of any social service.

It is necessary to look more closely at the relationship between interventions and outcomes and to see how far the design of an evaluative instrument can contribute to a better understanding of that connection. There are at least two matters to be considered. The first is the need for a theoretical framework within which child care interventions can be placed and the second is the relationship between what have been called 'intermediate' outcomes and 'final' outcomes.

I   The Need for a Theoretical Framework

There are a number of reasons why the analysis of the connection between interventions and outcomes would benefit from being set within a theoretical framework.

(i)   As we have seen, there are likely to be practical limitations to the design of any evaluative scheme. From a purist's point of view a system based upon the random allocation of cases would be the most desirable; but it is unlikely to be adopted. That being so, a conceptual framework is particularly valuable since it offers the opportunity to identify and control for some of the many extraneous factors that might affect outcome.

(ii)   In a similar fashion the availability of a theoretical framework can help to unravel the potential interconnectedness of the wide variety of factors that appear to shape outcomes in child care. It directs attention towards certain patterns of influence and away from others.

(iii)   There are causal and hierarchical connections between the different dimensions of child welfare and therefore between the corresponding outcome indicators. A clear conceptual framework can both help to identify these connections and also clarify which lower order achievements should or should not be viewed as outcomes in their own right.

(iv)   The 'care' that is provided by a social services department should not be considered in isolation but as an integral part of a service network which also encompasses education and health provision. Once again, however, it is well-nigh impossible to 'explain' how or why this or that outcome was realised without an organising framework that embraces the contributions and constraints of different parts of the relevant 'system'.

(v)   The fact that outcomes are specific to the contexts within which they occur may be too obvious to need pointing out. Nevertheless, it does emphasise the value of a theoretical framework which reflects the reality of those contexts and recognises their importance.

These are all somewhat technical reasons for advocating that outcomes in child care be set within a theoretical framework. The need to construct such a framework becomes even more apparent when the question of accountability is considered. Policies which are based upon an explicit set of principles and theoretical assumptions are capable both of being challenged against this frame of reference and of being evaluated against what actually occurs in practice. That does not mean to say that because policies are set within a theoretical framework they either can or should prescribe detailed remedies or courses of action. It does mean, however, as the term 'framework' implies, that these policy statements should incorporate a set of consistent propositions about the way in which, in general, objectives in child care can be realised through the interventions of the social services. Whereas in the past child care policy lacked discernible theoretical frameworks recent changes, not least the Children Act 1989, have begun to make good that deficiency.

II   Two Complementary Approaches

The 'production of welfare' approach that has been developed by the Personal Social Services Research Unit at the University of Kent (Davies and Knapp, 1981; Knapp, 1984) seemed to us to offer a useful way forward in conceiving the relationship between interventions and outcomes. There are five components to the model which forms the basis to this approach.

First, there is the idea of *final outcomes*. These are the kinds of concepts that we have been addressing throughout the preceding chapters: the changes in a child's welfare, defined along the dimensions spanned by society's general objectives for child care and child development. Secondly, there are *intermediate outcomes* which are measures of the quality of care rather than the quality of life: they would include a supportive environment, a caring and attentive parent and a secure and stable family. All are achievements in themselves (and hence outcomes), but none of them is desired for its own sake. Their relevance lies in their known or presumed effect on final outcome.

On the other side of the 'production relationship' are the inputs. *Resource inputs* are the conventional, tangible service resources, including staff, physical capital, provisions and other consumable items. Associated with the resource inputs are the *costs* of child care provision; these, when properly measured, can provide shorthand indicators of the extent of resources. In contrast, there are *non-resource inputs*. These are influences on final and intermediate outcomes which are embodied in the personalities, activities, attitudes and experiences of the principal people in the child care system: the social workers; the care staff; birth and substitute parents, and the children themselves. Obvious examples of non-resource inputs, therefore, are the characteristics of the social environment; the degree of control exercised by parents; the influence of peer groups; the strength of inter-personal relationships; the child's own level of physical and emotional development, and so on. However, it is not always clear how non-resource inputs are to be distinguished from certain intermediate outcomes.

The analogy of a 'production system' employed in this model is certainly not intended to suggest that the process is mechanistic or simple. For example, the extent to which any one group of factors influences an outcome will depend upon the way in which they are combined, upon the sequence in which they occur or are experienced and upon how critical a particular combination or single factor has become in the light of what has gone before. For instance, the consequences of the sudden death of a parent may differ according to the timing of other traumatic events that befall a child. Furthermore, the crucial question may not be how certain factors come together but what order (or magnitude) of change has to occur before a particular outcome is produced. There is evidence to suggest that in child care quite small shifts in this interactive process may have important repercussions.

Of course, there will always be a number of explanatory models to choose from and others can be contrived. Their theoretical underpinnings may or may not be similar. For example, the 'production of welfare' approach will inevitably steer social workers away from focusing on the pathological nature of the problems they confront towards an interactionist perspective. This could also be true in relation to the idea of 'competence' which has gained a good deal of currency in the child care field.

Psychologists define competence as a repertoire of skills and abilities which a person has at his or her disposal to deal with the environment in which they find themselves. Some theorists, such as Maluccio (1981), see the concept of competence in transactional terms; that is, as the outcome of the interplay between a person's abilities, his or her motivation, and certain qualities in the impinging environment that range from social networks to financial circumstances. The strengths of such an interactional model are well documented in many settings, such as school. Children with high abilities may show little competence if their motivation is low or if the environment is unsupportive, whilst highly motivated children of low or average abilities may achieve considerable competence in an encouraging environment. This dynamic view of the development of behaviour and feeling has important implications for the role of social work intervention in providing appropriate environmental opportunities through which people may be enabled to change. Even where people are obliged to function in environments that cannot be modified, this model is helpful in that it offers an explanation of inadequacy which counteracts the tendency to blame the victims.

'Competence' reflects the way in which a person's innate skills develop as motivation and opportunity allow. Even so, a person who has acquired a degree of competence may still only function effectively in certain contexts: in that case it should be the social worker's task to identify the factors which enable him or her to function well in some situations and to look for the means to carry these over to others. A distinction should be made between discrete competences which enable someone to perform specific skills and the broader transactional concept of competence which is more pervasive and which affects the nature of relationships of many kinds. Of course, the two versions interact, for the acquisition of specific skills is likely to improve people's image of themselves and this, in turn, contributes to an overall sense of competence.

The value of the notion of competence is that it highlights for the social worker what needs to be asked in a particular situation about a family, its members and their environment that might lead to interventions which enable it to function more effectively, both collectively and individually. Aldgate, Maluccio and Reeves' work (1989) provides a useful example. They have devised a means of rating the extent to which, on the reports of their carers, adolescents are considered to be prepared for adulthood. Foster parents are asked to rate the youngsters on a list of skills that are thought to be necessary for independent living.

These range from an ability to budget successfully to a capacity to sustain relationships. Likewise, foster parents of school children are, for example, asked a series of questions which are designed to ascertain how well a child is functioning in school. Although, clearly, there are different kinds and degrees of competence, and some children are more able than others, this approach concentrates on a child's strengths, focusing on the ways in which it might be possible to alter inappropriate or detrimental factors in the interaction between a child and his or her environment. Unless one believes that it is possible to create new contexts which might compensate a child for past disadvantages there is little hope of taking positive action.

We felt that the interactional perspective that was central to both the notion of the 'production of welfare' and to the idea of the 'nurture of competence' provided a basis from which a practical evaluative instrument might be devised. In somewhat different ways both models emphasise (and thereby acknowledge) the complicated interconnections between the factors upon which a particular outcome may turn. Each also draws attention to the importance of intermediate outcomes and hence suggests how the tasks of measuring and explaining results

quality of life for their children. There is, therefore, a presumed connection between the one and the other and hence an implicit 'explanation' for successful upbringing.

What is valuable about the notion of the reasonable parent is also that it can be applied to the manner in which a local authority with certain parental rights and duties fulfils its responsibilities. The good local authority will mirror the practices of the reasonable parent. By taking the practices of the reasonable parent as the yardstick for evaluating the performance of a local authority (or other corporate body with child care responsibilities) the emphasis is shifted away from rather intangible and elusive 'final outcomes' towards what is actually being done. Whether these actions are called 'intermediate outcomes' or 'inputs' is of less significance than that they should be accomplished and that that accomplishment should be checked by means of a practical assessment procedure.

One objection to the use of the 'reasonable parent' as a criterion for evaluating the performance of a local authority in its role as a child care agency may be that this approach takes insufficient account of the extent to which the needs of the children who come to the attention of public bodies are deeper and more far-reaching than the needs of those who do not. In that sense a local authority should be expected to go beyond what the ordinary reasonable parent would (or could) do. That certainly needs to be borne in mind, but it can also be argued that, faced with a child whose needs are profound, the reasonable parent *also* goes beyond what would normally be done, by seeking advice, help or special treatment.

Our argument has been that the difficulty of attributing certain results to certain interventions by local authorities is substantially reduced if we focus on intermediate rather than on overall or final outcomes. Of course, the distinction between the two is somewhat artificial, but it is nevertheless conceptually clear, having a good deal to do with when, in a sequence of events, the particular outcome in question is considered to occur. However, none of this is to say that the problem of explanation disappears or that it is unimportant. It still needs to be addressed by research if longer-term improvements are to be made in our understanding and thus in the practice of social work. In particular, any system of routine assessment of outcomes must be developed in association with a programme of such research, for only in that way will the many presumptions upon which any system of evaluation is obliged to rely be confirmed or refuted.

We have now examined many of the conceptual and theoretical issues that lie behind the production of reliable outcome measures. We have discussed why such measures should recently have been seen as necessary; we have considered the various perspectives, time-scales and comparison groups which they might employ; we have examined how outcomes might be evaluated, and we have discussed how they might be explained. We are almost ready to move from a general examination of the issues involved towards constructing specific measures, but before we do so, one further question needs to be addressed: whose outcomes will these measures be designed to assess? That question is considered in the following chapter.

Summary of the Main Points from this Chapter

1. The adoption of a theoretical framework within which outcomes can be assessed will make it easier to determine accountability. Policies will be more readily assessed, and practices will be simpler to evaluate if they can be referred to a specific frame of reference.

2. A production of welfare approach introduces the possiblity of examining final outcomes in terms of their relationship to intermediate outcomes or quality of experiences, and resource inputs.

3. Theories of competence emphasise the value of adopting an interactionist approach which examines how a child's strengths can be built upon and how new contexts can be created to compensate for past disadvantages.

4. The approach which we have adopted focuses on the adoption of parental responsibilities by local authorities (or other corporate bodies) and asks how far the care they provide matches up to what might be expected from a reasonable parent.

5. Accountability is seen to lie not so much in the final outcome as in the extent to which children are offered the type of experiences which are necessary (though not always sufficient) for success.

Chapter 5

Which Children?

Even when a theoretical framework for evaluating outcomes has been constructed, it will still be necessary to specify which group of children is to be assessed before an instrument can be designed which accurately measures their experiences. On the face of it this may appear to be a straightforward decision. Certainly, in the past the dividing line would have been drawn between children who were in the care of a local authority and those who were not. However, that simple distinction has become increasingly artificial as the work with children and their families engaged upon by social services departments has developed beyond the provision of substitute care. By the 1980s the 'child care service' had become a complicated, diverse and expanding set of activities that was no longer adequately defined in terms of responsibilities for the admission, placement and discharge of children 'in care'.

The Children Act 1989 has both recognised these changes and extended them. In particular, it places a new duty on local authorities to help all children in their area who are deemed to be 'in need'. Furthermore, when social services departments intervene in family life, either on a voluntary basis or through compulsory powers, there is a clear expectation that parental responsibilities will be shared with parents, although the balance will vary according to the nature and severity of the problem. Both of these features of the new Act increase the need to be clear about which children are to be included in any scheme for the measurement of child care outcomes. However, the confusion was not created by the Act; it already existed as a result of the changes in the child care service that occurred in the 1970s and 1980s and, in some cases, earlier.

I   The Artificiality of Administrative and Legal Categories

It is obviously misleading to limit an assessment of the children who are dealt with by the child care service to those who are regarded as being 'in care'. In the first place different social services departments pursue different policies and practices and these affect the number of children who fall into this or that category. The problems of some children who are not 'in care' in one area may be virtually indistinguishable from those who are 'in care' in another (Packman *et al.*, 1986). Likewise, some children come in and out of care on several occasions; whether they appear in an enumeration of the 'in care' population therefore depends upon when the counting is done.

Similarly, it is plain that many children who are not 'in care' are 'in need', however that condition be defined. Indeed, one of the surprising aspects of the 1980s has been the rapid decline in the number and rate of children 'in care' at a time when most conventional indices suggested that need was increasing. Unemployment has become commonplace, homelessness has increased and the relative incomes of the poor have diminished. Divorce and separation have continued at high levels and, partly as a result, the number of one-parent families has grown significantly. Against such a background it was hardly to be expected that the last decade would witness the 25 per cent reduction in the number of children in local authority care that occurred. Clearly there is no simple relationship between economic and social adversity and children coming into 'care'. 'Need' and 'care' are linked by a more subtle process than simple cause and effect.

There are a number of possible explanations for the unexpected downward trend in the 'in care' figures during the 1980s. First, in a time of financial retrenchment it is possible that local authorities tightened their criteria for the admission of children to 'care' in order to reduce costs. In that respect it is interesting to note that the fall in the number and rate of children 'in care' in the 1980s mirrored what happened in the late 1920s and early 30s when unemployment and cuts in public expenditure were at their height. Indeed, throughout this century the rate of children 'in care' has risen in times of economic prosperity and fallen during periods of economic decline. Such a pattern certainly suggests that the child care service has been supplyled rather than demand or need driven.

However, wider demographic changes could also have contributed to the downward trend in the number and rate of children 'in care'. Social services departments are now having to assist a much larger number of elderly people than ever before. Likewise, the movement of the mentally ill and mentally handicapped from hospitals to community settings has also introduced additional demands. Faced by such mounting pressures, local authorities are likely to seek economies in all their activities, irrespective of the precise level of need for any particular service.

Another explanation for the remarkable reduction in the number of children 'in care' in the 1980s rests upon the assumption that because of more preventive work the circumstances under which children are admitted to care, and subsequently returned home, have changed. What might once have been accepted as sufficient cause for taking a child into care may no longer be considered to justify such action, especially in the case of voluntary procedures.

The grounds for admission to 'care' have become more specific and more related to inter-personal problems in family relationships. For example, Wedge and Phelan (1987) reported that social workers ranked family and marital disruption and the emotional deprivation of parents far above unemployment, poor housing or low income as factors contributing to a child's admission to 'care'. Similarly, Packman et al. (1986) found that social workers regarded unemployment and poor housing as but part of the background against which the major contributory reasons for a child coming into 'care' operated. In short, therefore, it is apparent that ideas about the kinds of 'need' that warrant admission to 'care' are continually changing. Neither the size nor the composition of the group of children who have hitherto been classified as 'in care' have been determined by immutable definitions. Both have been shaped by an assortment of factors which have altered in response to changing social and economic circumstances as well as to new professional beliefs and practices.

Hence, it is inappropriate to restrict the measurement of outcomes in child care solely to children who are 'in care'. That population is inconsistently defined from place to place and from time to time and is, in any case, only a partial reflection of the work now undertaken by what are termed the child care services of the local authorities.

II   The Effect of the Children Act 1989

The introduction of the new Children Act makes it even more obvious that the evaluation of child care outcomes cannot be confined to the assessment of what happens to those children who have been described in the past as being 'in care'. Admittedly, a certain group will still be classed as being legally in the care of local authorities; but henceforth many more will be 'accommodated' on an informal basis by social services departments whilst others will be assisted by a variety of interventions that do not entail children leaving home. In line with these changes, ideas about the distribution of parental responsibilities are being reshaped and new duties are being placed upon local authorities to help all children in their areas who are deemed to be 'in need'.

The notion of 'parental responsibility' is central to the Act. This is conceived as 'the collection of duties, rights and authority which a parent has in respect of his child'. Furthermore, 'the duty to care for the child and raise him to moral, physical and emotional health' is seen as 'the fundamental task of parent-hood and the only justification for the authority it confers' (Department of Health, 1989a; p.1).

Normally, the birth parents would be expected to take full responsibility for their children; but where they are not both living with them, as in the case of divorce, the courts will have the power to decide how that responsibility is divided. There is a presumption that both parents will remain responsible even when they are separated. In short, as the official guide to the Act points out, 'interventions by the courts where there is a family breakdown should not be regarded as lessening the duty on both parents to continue to play a full part in the child's upbringing' (Department of Health, 1989a; p. 1).

However, the Act recognises that there are similarities between the situation of separated parents and the circumstances under which social services departments intervene in families' lives, either voluntarily in response to sudden misfortune, or com-pulsorily where children are at risk of harm. In all these instances the new legislation indicates that, wherever possible, parental responsibility should be shared between the parents, the care providers and the local authority—although the bal-ance will vary according to the nature and severity of the problem.

This concept of enduring parental responsibility, and the notion of the 'reasonable parent' have influenced our ideas about both the design of a practical means of outcome assess-ment and the definition of the group of children to whom it might be applied. We have assumed, quite straightforwardly, that any scheme should be built upon what reasonable parents would do in order to achieve the best for their children. However, this is not to deny that there are children whose problems or protection require additional help from the State. For example, in some cases where children have been neglected or abused such intervention will be called for precisely because parents have acted unreasonably; but in others, such as where a child suffers from a severe disability, the problems may be more than a 'reasonable' parent can cope with unaided. Of course, there is a wide range of problems, and also considerable overlap between them.

The Act therefore defines rather broadly the kinds of children who should be helped by social services departments, referring to them as a group of children 'in need'. According to the Act (sect. 17) a child is in need if:

(a) he is unlikely to achieve or maintain, or have the opportunity of achieving or maintaining, a reasonable standard of health or development without the provision for him of services by a local authority . . .

(b) his health or development is likely to be significantly impaired, without the provision for him of such services, or

(c) he is disabled.

Those children living away from home whose welfare must be safeguarded by the local authority would include all those who are 'accommodated by' or 'in the care of' a local authority, those in other establishments such as hospitals or boarding schools, and children in private foster homes. However, it is plain that the way in which need is defined extends a local authority's responsibilities to children living at home as well. In summary, therefore, children 'in need' will include all those with whom social services departments are in touch. If authorities take seriously the responsibility to identify all children in need in their areas this number will doubtless increase.

If, therefore, we take the new category of children in need as the group which should be subject to outcome evaluation the coverage will be extensive. In principle, this is to be welcomed; after all, children move between systems and may change their administrative or legal status several times before they reach adulthood. However, practical considerations are likely to dictate that the application of a scheme of outcome evaluation will be limited to a smaller group than this, at least at first. Nevertheless, the system should be designed in such a way that it is capable of being used for the most broadly defined group of children with whom social services departments are in touch.

This leads, for example, to the question of outcomes that lie beyond the end of any particular category of social services help. We know that, at present, the patterns of discharge from care are different from one area to another and, within an authority, from one locality to another. They also alter from year to year (Aldgate, 1976; Knapp *et al.*, 1985). If we are to assess how appropriate these different practices are, or how important post-care services may be, it is obviously wrong for the evaluation of outcomes to be restricted to set periods of this or that service. Moreover, the Children Act (sect. 24) allows authorities to adopt a more constructive approach than has hitherto been available to them in assisting and befriending youngsters who have left care or accommodation. If local authorities are to continue to offer a service to children whom they have once looked after, it follows that they should also continue to measure its effectiveness.

There are many other reasons why a scheme of outcome evaluation needs to be applicable to all children with whom local authorities are (or should be) in touch. For instance, some departments have adopted strategies which reduce the number of admissions on paper by placing certain residential services outside the care system. Thus, in some areas children may be offered respite accommodation without this being counted as a formal admission. In child protection cases, some authorities have tried to minimise the trauma of separation by placing children with 'safe' adults who are part of their day-to-day network. Sometimes specialist foster homes for adolescents offer a period of residence that is either a prelude to or instead of a placement 'in accommodation', and again the child is never formally admitted (Webb, 1990).

It is not known whether children (or parents) feel less stigmatised by such informal admissions; nor do we know to what extent frequent episodes of 'short-term' accommodation offer experiences similar to the respite services available to children with learning disabilities. There are no figures to show how many children who oscillate in and out of care would once have been the 'children who wait', now discharged prematurely to prevent them from languishing in the system. Although at the moment respite care is still not common (apart from children with learning difficulties) the new Act will almost certainly increase its use. The shift in philosophy towards the provision of temporary accommodation as a supporting service to prevent permanent breakdown in families makes it more important than ever for these types of placements to be seen as part of the planned long-term enhancement of children's welfare.

Respite care is just one of many services that have been conveniently grouped together as 'preventive'. That description covers a rich assortment of activities and has come to comprise a major part of the work of the child care services. Clearly the children for whom such services are provided are in touch with departments and therefore should be included in any evaluation of outcomes. So far the evaluation of these services in terms of their effect on children's lives has received little attention, although there has been a recent flurry of research. In particular, Gibbons' (1989) two-area study of community-based services has made an excellent contribution, while a theoretical framework for measuring the success of such services has been developed by Hardiker and her colleagues (1989). Any scheme that does not continue to build upon such initiatives to incorporate 'preventive' services into outcome evaluation would be sadly deficient.

III   The Promotion of Children's Welfare

The Children Act 1989 widens the duty which currently requires local authorities to consider the long-term welfare of all children in touch with the personal social services to include, as we have seen, children in the community who are deemed to be in need. This comprehensive definition of the duty to promote child welfare offers the chance to move away from the negative and narrow definition of child care as simply those activities that are concerned with children who are looked after by local authorities. It also provides the opportunity to escape from the equally negative assumption that the prevention of something undesirable occurring is a sufficient aim for the child care services.

In future, therefore, any system of outcome measurement must take account of how well a local authority's activities have promoted the positive well-being of a child. The painfully persistent legacy of minimum standards and minimum objectives that was inherited from the Poor Law must finally be shed. This will not happen, however, unless careful consideration is given to the question of how local authorities are to implement a 'promotional' philosophy and how, in its turn, this is to be reflected in the evaluation of their achievements.

It is heartening to find that both the wider definition of the group of children for assessment and the application of the principle of 'welfare promotion' facilitate the adoption of general rather than special criteria in evaluating the development of children 'in need'. On another level too the application of similar 'promotional' criteria both to children who remain at home and to those who are living apart from their families offers the opportunity of making important comparisons.

We have endeavoured to take account of the need to adopt a 'promotional' philosophy in the way that we have designed our prototype instrument for outcome assessment. The standards we set are intended to raise the low expectations that are too often held for disadvantaged children. As we have said, in the process of designing the measures, we found it helpful to think of how the idea of the 'reasonable parent', introduced by the Children Act, could be applied to the parent-like responsibilities that a local authority carries.

We have also given particular consideration to the question of how parents themselves can best be helped and encouraged to play as full a part as possible in promoting their children's well-being. One obvious step forward is to encourage further dialogue between professionals and parents about the type of inputs that research has shown are necessary for children's successful development. As will become clear in chapters 7 and 8, the method of assessment that we propose is designed both to raise consciousness about such issues and to encourage all those who are responsible for the care of children to participate in both the monitoring and the planning process.

In the next two chapters we describe in detail the instrument that we have devised for the measurement of child care outcomes and explain more fully the reasons that have lain behind its design. In chapter 6 we explain our choice of dimensions and show why we consider it necessary to monitor children's progress across such a wide spectrum. Chapter 7 describes how we constructed the schedules through which outcomes in each of these dimensions can be measured. We believe that use of the schedules will, in itself, help to develop the philosophies of 'reasonable' parenting, the active promotion of children's well-being and the emphasis on shared responsibility that are such central features of the new legislation.

Nevertheless, we appreciate that local authorities will find it extremely difficult to apply the schedules that we have devised to the fullest range of children 'in need' or 'in touch'. A start might be made with children looked after away from home but, as soon as possible, we hope that more categories will be included. As they stand the schedules can be incorporated into the statutory review process. If this is done they will provide a continuous means of monitoring children throughout the period of their involvement with social services departments. Certain design features have been introduced for this purpose; other modest changes might have to be made to facilitate their application in other circumstances. Nevertheless, we do wish to emphasise the general applicability of this instrument to a wide group of children described as 'in need' in the terms of the 1989 Act.

Summary of the main points from this chapter

1. The downward trend in the numbers of children 'in care' can be explained by several factors, but it does not reflect a reduction of the number of children 'in need'. The distinction between children who are looked after by local authorities and those who are not

is often an arbitrary one, and can alter from time to time and from place to place.

2. The duty laid on local authorities by the Children Act 1989 to safeguard and promote the welfare of children in need, together with the expectation that parents will share in the responsibility for children who are looked after away from home have blurred the arbitrary distinction between being 'in care' and not being 'in care'.

3. Although practical considerations may initially limit assessments to the group of children who are looked after away from home, any means of evaluating child care outcomes should be capable of covering the wider group of children 'in need' who receive 'preventive' services designed to enhance their long-term welfare.

4. The new, positive duty to promote children's welfare should finally overcome the last traces of a policy of less eligibility, inherited from the Poor Law. A system of evaluation should reflect promotional policies by setting standards that are intended to raise expectations for children in need. It should also help and encourage parents to take an active part in promoting and monitoring their children's welfare.

Chapter 6

Identifying the Dimensions for Assessment

I Towards a Broader Perspective on Child Welfare

In this chapter we take a step towards translating the principle of welfare promotion embodied in the Children Act 1989 into a framework for assessment of outcomes and improvement of practice. We begin by setting out the argument for a multi-dimensional view of children's development and well-being. We suggest that placement, though clearly of great importance, should be seen as only one aspect of the social worker's task, to be set alongside the continuing work of monitoring the quality of care provided for the child on a range of different dimensions. The second part of the chapter explains in more detail the reasons for selecting particular dimensions for inclusion in the assessment process, and briefly reviews the research evidence on which the choice was based.

As we have noted already, outcomes in child care tend to be defined mainly in negative terms; that is, as the avoidance of problems rather than as the achievement of positive objectives. This is partly explained by the fact that it is much easier for people of different social classes and ethnic groups to agree on undesirable outcomes. Almost no parents are indifferent to their children's ill-health, unemployment, poor education, inability to form stable relationships or dependence on drugs or alcohol. Furthermore, negative outcomes can often be expressed in terms of incidents such as placement breakdown, taking an overdose, or committing an offence. By contrast, positive outcomes are more a matter of states of being, ranged along a continuum, so that the point at which a particular child is located involves a judgement.

That being so, those who assess the outcome of care for a particular child as being good or bad may have quite different concepts in mind. This becomes clear if we take a historical perspective. At one time it was an achievement if a child survived infancy; all that was required of the State was the provision of physical care, food and shelter at a minimum level, followed by early discharge to some form of employment. In the wake of the Curtis report of 1946 and the development of a social work-based child care profession, the focus shifted to children's emotional experiences and relationships. During this formative period psychoanalytic theory was still the basis of much social work thinking and the influence of Bowlby (1951) was pervasive. Theories of attachment came to dominate child care policy in Britain and the United States in a way that did not happen in other countries, such as France or Israel. The effects of a theoretical orientation based upon the concept of attachment can still be seen today in the fact that the continuity of a placement is frequently considered to be one of the most important outcomes in child care. Ironically, this seems to be the very outcome which is most difficult to achieve. The histories of almost all children who spend more than a few months being looked after by a local authority are chequered with moves, transfers and discontinuities of all kinds (Millham et al., 1986).

A one-dimensional view of outcome is generally unhelpful and can narrow work with children and their families in ways which exclude important opportunities for making progress. For example, in her research on residential homes, Whitaker found that 'planning' for a child almost always concerned the question of his or her placement (1985). The plan, or the desired outcome for the child, was often to be placed with a foster family; but it might be months or years before a suitable family was found. During that time there were many intermediate goals that could have been achieved or worked for had there not been such a preoccupation with a single form of 'outcome'.

In this chapter we argue that a multidimensional view of outcome is needed in order to reflect the fact that a child's experience of being looked after by a local authority is likely to have both positive and negative aspects which produce a mixture of gains and losses. Disaggregating the concept of outcome is helpful at the level of the individual child in that it ensures that his or her needs and development are looked at in detail and that plans are related to the present situation, and not all focused upon some more distant achievement. At the management and planning level, identifying the different components of outcome can help to draw attention to weaknesses and gaps in the service. Linked to this is the need to increase and standardise the basic minimum of information collected by social workers, to raise their awareness of certain issues and to modify recording habits.

There is a natural tendency for social workers to be preoccupied with those issues that appear to be of greatest topical importance. For example, they are likely to read more and attend more conferences and meetings about AIDS than about motor cycle accidents, even though the latter are currently a much greater hazard to young people. Similarly, there is more concern about minor delinquency in adolescence than about alcohol dependency; and the sexual abuse of children attracts infinitely more attention than child poverty. In other words, without a clearly articulated selection of outcomes on a number of well-chosen dimensions, the preoccupations of the moment may assume a greater importance than other equally significant matters that remain in comparative obscurity.

How then should the dimensions on which we assess outcome be chosen? One possible criterion, as we have noted, is public expectation. There is, for example, some agreement as to minimum standards. Families which fail to provide an acceptable level of care may find that social workers are authorised to intervene in an otherwise private area of their lives and, in extreme cases, remove their children.

However, beyond that, an examination of public expectations of child care reveals a shifting picture on which it would be hard to base any systematic assessment scheme. For instance, two principles appear to exist side by side. On the one hand the whole child care system, and public attitudes towards it, are still influenced by vestiges of the old Poor Law principle of less eligibility; that is the notion that children who are looked after by a local authority away from home should not be better off then those in similar social circumstances who remain with their parents. This depresses expectations because so many children 'in care' come from poor families suffering multiple stresses and low standards of living (Holman, 1980). On the other hand, there is the principle of normalisation; namely, that children looked after by a local authority should be as indistinguishable as possible from those growing up in an 'average' family. Of course, there are many ideas about what constitutes an average family, but it is certainly assumed (in the developed world at least) that the adults in such a family will be able to provide the children with adequate food, bedding, clothing and security, as well as with activities similar to those enjoyed by most other children of the same age. Although there has been a shift from the first to the second of these positions, at least among social workers, an uneasiness about providing too high a standard of care for children looked after by a local authority lingers on, particularly in relation to education, as we argue below. The conflict of attitudes and values is well illustrated by an incident that was reported in a study of a residential children's home (Jackson, 1988, 1989). The officer in charge was strongly committed to the idea of normalisation. Finding that the children in the home were wearing a mixed assortment of shabby shoes, he took them all to a sports shop and bought them trainers, such as were currently being worn for school by other children. Each child was encouraged to choose the make and type he or she wanted. This action horrified the older members of staff. No doubt when they took their own children shopping they were as subject to the vagaries of their likes and dislikes as any other parents; but that fashion should play any part in how these children were clothed seemed to them quite inappropriate, indeed a prodigal waste of public and charitable funds.

An Interdisciplinary Approach
It is probably inevitable that the two principles will continue to co-exist in any system of child care provided by the State as a substitute for, or, in the philosophy of the Children Act 1989, as a supplement to what is offered by natural parents. However, if we are aiming for quality in child care perhaps we should take as our guide the classic statement of the Hadow report in 1931: 'What a wise and good parent would desire for his own children that a nation must desire for all children'. Of course, not many people now would be so confident in assuming that we all know what is 'wise and good'. We are aware of the numerous different meanings that phrase might have for people of different social classes or ethnic backgrounds. Nevertheless, the perspective that Hadow's statement represents is illuminating. By directing attention to the role of the State as parent it underlines the weakness of looking at a child's progress from a single professional viewpoint. The fact that social work is the profession with responsibility for child care has tended to produce a distorted picture of outcome, with the focus being on what concerns social workers rather than on the overall development of the child. For the social worker, the continuance of a placement is an overriding preoccupation. Studies of social work decision-making show, for example, that child care workers tend to disregard health and education as being matters for the attention of other professions (Knapp et al., 1985), whereas most parents give them a high priority. If the aim in child care is to emulate good parenting, clearly an inter-disciplinary approach to the determination and assessment of outcome is essential.

Promoting Welfare
Retrospective accounts by people who have been 'in care' suggest that undesirable outcomes often occur by default rather than as a result of deliberate policy (Kahan, 1979). Children's lives may be as deeply affected by the actions that child care workers fail to take as by what they actually do (Fisher et al., 1986). In general, social workers concentrate on trying to avert negative outcomes, or on picking up the pieces after they have

occurred, rather than on acting to promote the conditions which may lead to positive results.

By some kind of transmutation, the absence of a negative outcome may be seen by social workers and social service managers as a positive achievement, and in a sense this may be valid if other children in care are taken as the comparison group. If, instead, the child looked after by a local authority is compared with the general population of children, a very different perspective is brought to bear, and one which may well reveal the extent to which children 'in care' are falling below their potential. One way to overcome the problem of low expectations is to analyse outcomes by using dimensions that are applicable to any child and which would be considered important by most parents. However, it cannot be denied that children looked after by local authorities do have particular problems and difficulties. The selection of significant dimensions should also include those areas which research has shown to be especially problematic for these children.

In the light of all these considerations we recommend that seven dimensions should be incorporated in the assessment of outcome for children who are or who have been looked after or supervised by a local authority. Although some of these dimensions will not form part of the reason why the local authority is involved in the care of the child, all will need to be assessed if the adequate fulfilment of parental responsibilities is to be regarded as the ultimate purpose of child care interventions. The dimensions are:

> Health
> Education (including skills training and employment in the older age groups)
> Emotional development and behaviour
> Social, family and peer relationships
> Self-care and competence
> Identity
> Social presentation

The decision to choose these as the key dimensions for assessment was reached by first listing a number of areas that were considered on the basis of research findings to be of particular significance to children's development at specific ages. The areas chosen for four-year-olds, for example, were: 'physical development', 'intellectual development', 'management expectations' (self-care skills), 'social expectations', 'public acceptability', 'play' and 'family relationships'. Additional dimensions were then chosen for older children: 'educational achievements', 'independence' and 'involvement of services' were added to the list when the child reached eight. By the time children reached eighteen, the number of dimensions had increased to sixteen. On close scrutiny, however, it became evident that many of these more specialised categories could be collapsed to form broader dimensions that are of significance to all children of all ages. For example, 'intellectual development', 'play' and 'educational achievements' were all seen to be aspects of a broader educational dimension.

It seems unlikely that the list of seven dimensions that we propose as necessary components of an all-round assessment of outcome could be further reduced or amalgamated without diminishing the quality of the measures used. It can, however, be seen that these dimensions are not all of the same order. Some lend themselves to objective measurement, others can only be assessed subjectively. Some dimensions will assume greater significance than others at different periods in a child's life, although we would argue that they are all relevant at some level throughout childhood. For example, babies have educational needs as well as ten-year-olds; children are beginning to have a sense of their own identity by the age of two; and older adolescents seem to require much more practical and emotional support than is often assumed.

Should all the dimensions carry equal weight? Surely, some are more central to what might be seen as a 'good' outcome? The research evidence does not provide much support for this view. Rather it seems that the different dimensions interweave and interact with each other. Parents appear to keep all of them in mind even though they may intervene more actively in particular areas at particular times. For this, and for other reasons discussed in chapter 3, we have not attempted to produce a hierarchy of outcome dimensions.

Of course, there is some artificiality in treating as separate entities what are really different facets of a child's life and development. It is often necessary to make an arbitrary decision whether a certain aspect should be included in one dimension rather than another. Should substance abuse, for instance, be considered as a health or a behavioural problem? Moreover, it is clear that there are no firm boundaries between dimensions, so that a developmental feature which has been categorised in one way may interact to influence what happens in other spheres. Inadequate self-care skills may result in poor self-presentation; inappropriate behaviour may affect education or health, and so on. Nonetheless, some system of classification is necessary and we believe that what we have devised reflects the conclusions of much relevant research and that it is also sympathetic to what might be termed the common sense of parenting.

II   Selecting Dimensions for Assessment

In this section we consider the justification for believing the seven recommended dimensions to be important elements in achieving a satisfactory outcome for children looked after by local authorities. One useful by-product of this exercise has been to reveal aspects of children's experience and development where there is a lack of relevant research and it is hoped that the classification of dimensions adopted here may help to stimulate research interest in overlooked topics. We do not suggest that other areas are necessarily unimportant, but some balance has to be struck between comprehensiveness and achieving a process of assessment on a manageable scale. The seven dimensions are reviewed in turn.

Health
All social classes and ethnic groups give high priority to keeping their children physically healthy. Indeed, it could be seen as the basic parental task. Blaxter (1981) and Mayall (1986)

have both shown that a heavy responsibility is carried by parents, mostly mothers, for monitoring and promoting children's health, with only occasional help from professionals. Many shortcomings are related far more to poverty, poor housing conditions and lack of resources than to indifference or ignorance. The effective health care that most parents provide for their children is related to their intimate daily contact with them, and is generally learned by experience. Because they know the child so well most parents are aware of the significance of small changes in appearance or behaviour in the context of the child's health history, and can take appropriate action immediately. They also have ideas about what they need to do to promote the child's health, even if material circumstances prevent them from doing everything that they would like.

When a child is looked after by a local authority these responsibilities pass in full or in part to a public body: a number of problems then arise. First, there is the problem of knowledge, both factual and intuitive, about the child's medical history and normal state. Then there is the division of responsibility between social worker and foster carer or residential social worker. No one person may see it as their job to carry out the daily monitoring which most parents do without thinking. Thirdly, the active promotion of health and health education may not be on anybody's agenda. These points will be discussed more fully in the following chapter.

Children 'in care' often come from disadvantaged sections of the population and are therefore at greater risk than others of suffering poor health (Court, 1976; Townsend and Davidson, 1982; Wedge and Essen, 1982; Blaxter, 1987; NCB, 1987). For example, in her study Mayall (1986) found that children from social classes III, IV and V were far more likely to suffer from persistent medical conditions than those in classes I and II (34 per cent as against 18 per cent), and twice as likely to have had three or more episodes of illness during the three months before the survey. It is possible, then, that many children coming into 'care' are in a relatively poor state of health. Acute illnesses will obviously provoke action; but chronic conditions may go unobserved and untreated. Detailed medical histories are rarely taken at admission and, in their absence, there may be nobody who can recognise the warning signs that a persistent condition is about to flare up. The child will often be treated by an unknown doctor and it may be impossible to answer relevant questions.

It is significant that we were able to find very few studies of the health of children in care, nor is the subject given prominence in the general child care literature. However, an analysis of data from the National Child Development Study by Lambert (1983) found that this group of children had many health problems. We also have some clues from observations made incidentally in the course of research that focuses on other areas. For example, uncorrected squints, crooked teeth and obesity have been remarked on, especially among children in residential care.

Social workers appear to appreciate the importance of dental check-ups and of carrying out recommended treatment when this is brought to their attention (see chapter 8). However the much longer timescale involved in orthodontic care and the need for constant parental monitoring create difficulties which are rarely overcome. Even if orthodontic treatment is started it may lapse if there is a change of placement.

Obesity may be related both to the child's pre-care experiences and to the current regime. Some children may come from families living in extreme poverty which have simply been unable to give them enough to eat, so that when suddenly moved to a setting where food is plentiful they are unable to regulate their intake. Indeed, if their experience of meals is erratic and unpredictable they may feel that they should eat as much as possible while it is on offer.

There are of course many other causes of obesity, genetic, psychological and practical; but one significant factor must be the diet offered in the care setting. A study of the menus provided over several months in a large voluntary children's home showed them to be entirely uninfluenced by current ideas about healthy eating (Jackson, 1989). Fresh fruit and vegetables rarely appeared, pasta, rice and pulses never. Meat, included in most meals, was often processed, bread was always white, and there was a heavy reliance upon frozen and packaged foods with a high fat and sugar content. There is no way of knowing if this is typical since there has been no systematic study of the diet provided for children in care. It is significant that whereas those in the social work world seem to have little interest in the matter, food and feeding are usually one of the central concerns of mothers, even though poverty may prevent them from offering their children a healthy diet. It is also a matter of great interest to young people themselves (Gardner, 1987).

It is likely that children coming into 'care' will already be accustomed to instant energy foods that are high in sugar and fat. Mayall (1986) has noted that the diet of children from social classes IV and V tends to deteriorate as they get older. A Department of Health survey (1989) of the diets of British schoolchildren found that this was true for boys but not for older girls. However, girls aged 10 to 11 from social class V ate nearly three times as many chips as those from social class I with similar trends towards sugar and sweets and away from fruit juice and vegetables. Failure to take positive action to change unhealthy eating habits is likely to have serious long-term consequences, increasing for instance the risk of coronary heart disease in middle age.

This issue has been discussed in some detail because it illustrates a number of points relevant to the selection of the dimensions along which outcomes have to be traced. First, it shows the danger of considering outcome from a single professional viewpoint by comparison with the multidimensional outlook of parents. Secondly, it is a good example of the way dimensions interact. Children who have chronically runny noses or are overweight are likely to be less attractive to adults and peers. This will adversely affect their self-presentation, social relationships and sense of self-esteem. An informed attitude to health care, prevention and promotion is related to high standards of self-care and competence. Thirdly, the example of diet demonstrates some of the difficulties that might arise in the choice of certain elements in a developmental dimension, for food is an important area of cultural difference. Great care needs to be exercised, therefore, in determining precisely how a 'satisfactory' diet is to be described in terms of its component foodstuffs and modes of preparation, even though the underlying principles of healthy eating may be widely applicable.

Education

If their children's health is of predominant concern to parents, education might come next on their list, for the good reason that it is so closely related to quality of life in adulthood. In many countries good education is regarded as a crucial outcome for children separated from their families; and 'care' is often located within the education system. However, in English-speaking countries—Britain, the United States, Canada and Australia—educational outcomes have often been overlooked (Jackson, 1987).

There is a large body of evidence about the relationship between education and life chances, particularly for children from very deprived backgrounds (Rutter, Quinton and Liddle, 1983; Pilling, 1987). On the other hand, there are many indications that at present children's education is given a low priority by child care social workers in Britain. Retrospective accounts by people who have grown up 'in care' frequently complain about the lack of attention given to their schooling (Kahan, 1979; Jackson, 1986). A large-scale study in Suffolk which looked at the relationship between social workers' stated objectives and their attainment found that although half the children were assessed as having school-related difficulties, educational improvement was only considered to be a specific aim for six of them. In all, only 16 out of 285 'objectives' listed by social workers related to education (Knapp et al., 1985).

This contrasts markedly with the attitudes of concerned parents. Parents in a position to choose are preoccupied with their children's schooling, often subordinating their own interests in the process. Estate agents advertise houses as being in districts with good schools, knowing that this will be an important selling point. Parents may refuse good jobs or live apart for a time so as not to disrupt their children's education.

Moreover, it has long been known that educational achievement is highly correlated with parental interest (Douglas, 1964) and information has been accumulating about how that interest is expressed in the day-to-day care of children. There is evidence from three major British longitudinal studies, as well as from the smaller but more detailed study of Nottingham children carried out by the Newsons, about the kinds of parenting practices which are likely to lead to educational success for children (Newson and Newson, 1977). These are by no means adopted by middle-class parents alone, although greater resources may enable them to promote their children's education more effectively. A recent study by Tizard and her colleagues (1988) found that 80 per cent of parents, mainly working class, thought that the choice of the child's first school was important, and over half had visited or considered schools other than the one the child finally attended. Pre-school literacy and numeracy were related to parental teaching independent of social class. The child's progress in infant school was strongly influenced by the amount of parental contact with, and knowledge about the school, again independent of social class.

Children looked after by a local authority suffer from a number of interlocking educational disadvantages. Some are 'external' such as the experience of frequently disrupted schooling and the lack of opportunities to acquire basic skills. Others are psychological, such as low self-esteem. However, a crucial factor seems to be the minimal expectations of social workers and care-givers about what children in their care are capable of achieving and the low priority that educational matters are accorded. Such attitudes permeate the care system, symbolised by the fact that the responsible government department requires no statistics on the school-leaving qualifications of children who may have spent their whole lives 'in care' and that local authorities do not systematically collect this information. Yet schools and parents are actively concerned, some might argue to an unreasonable degree, with the results of public examinations, and this in turn reflects their importance in determining future opportunities.

Education is not of course confined to school achievement. It includes the acquisition of skills such as riding a bicycle, swimming, playing a musical instrument and the development of individual special interests. As we have noted, Rutter and his colleagues found that the acquisition of skills improved children's self-confidence, thereby enabling them to proceed to further achievements (Rutter, Quinton and Liddle, 1983).

In the older age-groups the education dimension also includes training and employment. The unemployment level among young people who have been 'in care' is extraordinarily high (Millham et al., 1986; Stein and Carey, 1986). It has been argued that in times of generally high unemployment, not having a job can no longer be considered a negative indicator of outcome. However, the poor educational record of young people who are or have been looked after by a local authority away from home must adversely affect their chances of employment. Indeed, qualifications may be especially important for them since they are liable to lack the informal contacts and relationships which often produce jobs for young people living with their families. Employment encourages self-esteem, provides a clear sense of identity, and helps young people to develop skills in social relationships and self-presentation. Conversely, unemployment leads to a range of negative side-effects such as mental and physical ill-health (Smith and Jacobson, 1990, Smith, 1987), and probably an increased risk of offending.

Children looked after by a local authority experience little informed vocational guidance or career planning. Many social workers seem to take it for granted that they have nothing better to look forward to on leaving care than unemployment, albeit intermixed with periods spent on training projects or in temporary or occasional work. Many young people who would otherwise be unemployed might benefit from further education, but few social services departments at present exercise their powers to provide financial support for this purpose after the age of eighteen.

There are strong arguments, then, for social workers to give a far higher priority to the educational dimension (defined in its broadest sense) in their work with children 'in care'. To do this they will need to regard care or accommodation as a resource for providing compensatory services rather than as a means of preventing further damage. This appears to be the direction indicated by the underlying philosophy of the Children Act 1989.

Emotional and Behavioural Development
There is, unfortunately, copious evidence for the prevalence of emotional and behavioural problems among children 'in care', and this is the only dimension for which the evaluation focuses on negative outcomes. Emotional and behavioural problems may be the trigger which propels children into care in the first place. They are often a contributory cause of placement break-down and interact to damaging effect with other areas of children's lives (Lambert, Essen and Head, 1977; Osborn and St. Claire, 1987).

Behavioural problems are frequently manifestations of emotional stress; they may be a normal reaction to some of the disruptive events which children 'in care' too often suffer. We also need to recognise that these children are more subject to 'public' scrutiny than those growing up in their own homes. Sometimes what is seen as problematic by care-givers may be not much different from typical child or adolescent behaviour but is simply more obvious and troublesome to adults because of the special control that they are expected to exercise over children who are not their own. This type of problem can be amplified and reinforced by over-reaction. On the other hand, emotional and behavioural problems arising from threatening life events, unless sensitively treated, can become established and persist long after the original situation has receded into the past.

There is a clear connection between behavioural and emotional problems and poor school performance, a relationship which appears to operate both ways. Children who are withdrawn and depressed or preoccupied with worries cannot concentrate on their schoolwork. On the other hand, children who lack basic skills such as reading may behave badly in school either because they are unable to follow the work of the class and therefore become bored, or in order to mask their sense of failure. They may also be desperately seeking the attention they lack (Hoghughi, 1978; Demitri, 1982).

Emotional and behavioural development obviously overlap most of the other dimensions discussed in this chapter. Although there has been a reaction against the determinism implied in some of the writings of, for instance, Bowlby and Erikson, the damage caused by instability of care, especially in the early years, is obvious to anyone who has worked with children. This does not of course mean that care cannot be shared on a daily basis between a number of people (Schaffer, 1984; Melhuish and Moss, 1991), but there is no doubt of the high emotional risk attached to disrupting significant relationships. Behavioural responses may vary depending on the child's temperament—some children are far more resilient than others and better able to adapt to change (Thomas and Chess, 1977). Others may react either with overt hostility, apathetic withdrawal or a range of neurotic symptoms, of which bedwetting is one of the most common and tiresome for caregivers. One long-term consequence may be a failure to internalise a sense of basic trust in adult good intentions (Erikson, 1963) which may manifest itself later as chronic suspiciousness, amounting in severe cases to paranoia. This in turn can make relationships with authority figures such as teachers and employers extremely difficult and precarious (Jackson, 1987; Stein, 1990).

Anger, resentment and anxiety are often normal reactions to the experiences which bring children into the care system as well as to some of those imposed by the system itself. Examples of the latter would be separation for administrative reasons from people with whom a child has formed strong affectional bonds, failure to understand or listen to a child, or unacceptable practices in care settings, such as these revealed by the enquiry into Staffordshire children's homes (Levy and Kahan, 1991).

Behavioural and emotional development may be impaired by any of these experiences, but generally become a problem to others when a child's negative feelings are uncontrollable and cannot be expressed in a socially acceptable way. Reactions may be generalised so that trivial incidents provoke responses inappropriate in intensity or duration. For example temper tantrums in response to minor frustrations might be evaluated as normal in a two-year-old but a cause for serious concern in a child of ten. Similarly, irritability and bouts of dejection are not uncommon in adolescence but prolonged periods of depression and/or attempts to relieve it by the misuse of drugs or alcohol obviously call for expert help.

It is important to include behavioural and emotional development as a dimension for assessment since many children are looked after by local authorities because they have difficulties in these areas which their families and schools are unable to contain. In such cases the persistence of these problems, or their disappearance, are significant indicators of outcome. However, it should be emphasised that when attention to these issues reveals problems they ought not to be regarded as inevitable concomitants of 'care' but rather as conditions which may be amenable to skilled treatment.

Family and Peer Relationships
Social workers would probably see themselves as especially concerned with this area. Indeed, a great deal of the child care literature is devoted to questions of relationship. Closer examination, however, shows that the focus is surprisingly narrow, according overwhelming importance to the relationship with the mother or mother substitute—perhaps again reflecting the influence of Bowlby. However, once a child is separated from his or her birth family there is much evidence that rather low priority is given to facilitating contact even when it is considered desirable. Social workers sometimes believe, often mistakenly, that continuing contact with natural parents will jeopardise a new placement. Thus before the implementation of the Children Act 1989, *de facto* terminations of access were common (Bullock, Hosie, Little and Millham, 1991). Social workers' visits to natural parents tend to decline steeply over time, a factor which is strongly associated with foster home

breakdown (Berridge and Cleaver, 1987). As social workers reduce their contacts with natural parents, parents find it harder to remain in touch with their absent children.

The importance of maintaining links not only with mothers and fathers but also with a wider network of relatives and friends is also frequently overlooked, with the result that children may become 'lost in care' and leave in late adolescence with no adult support at all (Millham *et al.*, 1986). This dimension therefore needs to be interpreted much more broadly than simply as a child's interaction with his or her immediate care-givers, a point which is reinforced by the provisions of the Children Act 1989.

Another problem that has been identified in this area is the tendency to take a short-term view of relationships. One of the main problems for children 'in care' is the lack of continuity. There is a need for someone with a historical perspective, a 'reliable, caring adult', who is not necessarily providing day-to-day care or accommodation, but who can see particular incidents—a delinquent act, say—in the context of the child's whole lifetime. This relates to the point that is repeated over and over in first-hand accounts of growing up 'in care'; that a child does not just need a place to stay until he or she reaches adulthood, but a family for life (Triseliotis, 1980b). Social workers sometimes assume that this has to be the nuclear family or a substitute for it, even though many of the children they try to help come from cultures with a different definition of functioning family units and appropriate networks.

Gradually, we are becoming aware that the extended family is important to children who are looked after away from their immediate family group. In particular, grandparents may play an influential part in their lives and in shaping the wider pattern of family relationships that affect children. Farmer and Parker's (1991) study of children going home on trial, as well as Bullard and Malos's work on custodianship (1991), both highlight the crucial roles which may be played by grandparents, and some-times aunts, uncles and grown-up brothers and sisters.

We know very little about the relations of children 'in care' with their siblings. A high proportion of those coming into accommodation or care have brothers and sisters, who may or may not be in placements themselves (Rowe *et al.*, 1989; Parker, 1988). Some social workers make great efforts to keep siblings together or to see that they have regular contact if they are placed apart. Retrospective evidence suggests that this is very important and that for children in care to lose touch with their brothers and sisters is a sad and undesirable outcome (Wedge and Mantle, 1991). Brothers and sisters can offer valuable support to each other, if only in sharing adversity; contact with siblings preserves a sense of belonging which, when lost, may turn into feelings of betrayal and be reflected in behavioural and emotional problems.

Children who grow up 'in care' may also form lasting friendships outside the family which can provide a source of support when they leave. This is yet another neglected area. In contrast to parents, social workers do not appear to be able, or perhaps willing, to promote or discourage particular friendships or to widen children's social networks. We know however that friendships become of increasing significance as children grow older (Berndt and Ladd, 1989). The dominance of the peer group in adolescence is common knowledge. It may be especially important for children looked after by local authorities to have friends outside the care system, and this is something which could be consciously encouraged.

Thus, the maintenance or creation of a supportive, affectionate and reliable network of relationships is an important outcome in child care. In the past that network has tended to be perceived rather narrowly by social workers and carers. Its cultivation and improvement have been restricted largely to the close family. Clearly, the State as parent should be concerned with a wider range of social relationships for a child in its care, for these can help to provide opportunities and continuity, enhance self-esteem and personal identity as well as nurture the sense of being cherished and valued. Of course, some relationships may be detrimental; but we return to the point that the 'reasonable' parent would endeavour to steer a child away from such liaisons by contriving others, by example and sometimes by subterfuge. A local authority through its social workers or carers may not be able to do as much; but it cannot ignore the issue. It has to take some responsibility for trying to shape the pattern of relationships experienced by a child in its care in ways that are generally regarded as beneficial (Quinton and Rutter, 1988).

Self-care and Competence
Children growing up in their own families are gradually given greater responsibility for looking after themselves, their living space, their clothes and possessions and making decisions about how to spend time and money, even though different families and ethnic groups vary in how independent they expect children of different ages and sexes to be. Young adults on the point of leaving home normally expect to take responsibility for most aspects of their lives, but the majority will continue to look to their families for a considerable amount of emotional and material support.

However, studies of young people leaving care at the age of eighteen show them to be vulnerable and unsupported, expected to manage on their own and ill-equipped to do so (Stein, 1990). If they have spent a long time in a residential setting they may have had no chance to acquire practical domestic skills and be accustomed to constant supervision and little privacy. Then, suddenly, they find themselves in their late teens, or even earlier, in an isolated bedsitter, expected to manage their cooking, washing, cleaning and budgeting, all on a very low income. It is hardly surprising that so many young people who have spent part of their lives in care are to be found amongst the homeless or the prison population (Bullock *et al.*, 1990; Little, 1990).

Authorities which take these problems seriously have set up independence units to enable young people to practise the skills that they will need in order to manage on their own during the six months or so before they have to find their own way in the world. However, this is far too short a time to acquire the kind of competence which young people living with their families build up slowly over many years. Without the network of family support which most children and adolescents enjoy, youngsters in care need exceptional skills in order to cope with everyday living, not to mention the special adversities which they are likely to face. That is why self-care and competence are relevant at all ages, not just in later adolescence. 'Reasonable' parents would certainly be at pains to ensure that their children acquired these skills; indeed, many of them are seen as important yardsticks against which the developmental progress of younger children can be assessed. Likewise, teachers will expect children of certain ages to be able to manage certain tasks. The child who has not mastered them will be at a disadvantage and may fail to benefit fully from the school experience.

Identity

A few years ago the dimension of 'identity' might not have merited consideration; but child care workers have become increasingly aware of how essential a secure sense of identity is to children's well-being. Not only do children need to know who they are and where they have come from but to understand, as far as their age allows, why they are being looked after away from home. Knowledge about oneself and one's history is an important component of identity, as is generally recognized by the common practice of constructing life-story books with children. Ignorance can have damaging results. Berridge and Cleaver illustrate this vividly in one of their case histories of foster home breakdown. They describe how Paul, in his first year of secondary school, discovered by chance that a boy in the final year was his brother Geoff, of whose existence he was unaware, although Geoff was also in a social services foster home. When the story got about the school, Paul became an object of derision, and his resulting unhappiness probably contributed indirectly to the eventual failure of his foster placement (Berridge and Cleaver, 1987). Children need to be able to explain their situation to others in an acceptable way; this has crucial implications for how they think about themselves and especially for their self-esteem. Social identity is another component of a child's self-image which needs to be considered.

Of course, it is much harder to translate a relatively nebulous idea like the enhancement of identity into specific actions by social workers or carers than it is to ensure that a child's health is well looked after. However, enabling children to develop a positive self-concept is another of those basic tasks of parenting which happen naturally in most families but need much more thought in 'care' situations. Low self-esteem appears to be an underlying factor in many of the emotional and behavioural problems typically exhibited by separated children and is strongly associated with, for example, self-destructive behaviour in teenage girls, chronic mistrustfulness and poor educational achievement (Hoghughi, 1978).

Social identity is too complex a topic to explore in any detail here, but there is no doubt of its importance in shaping behaviour and attitudes (Hogg and Abrams, 1988). The Children Act 1989 attempts to reduce the stigmatizing effect of being looked after away from home by abolishing the 'in care' category, but this may not work entirely to the children's advantage if it condemns them to even greater isolation. Being able to identify with others in a similar situation and with similar problems can be a source of strength and increased self-esteem, as is demonstrated by the success of the magazine *Who Cares?* and the National Association for Young People in Care (NAYPIC). On the other hand there is evidence that outcomes tend to be more favourable for those who define themselves as members of more advantaged social groups, so that carers need to create situations in which this can be a possibility. The importance of encouraging children to make friends outside the care system has already been mentioned.

Black and mixed-race children have the additional problem that although they are over-represented in the care population the care system itself is overwhelmingly white, with still only a sprinkling of black social workers and care staff. It has been suggested that if they have no black adults with whom to identify, black children 'in care' may form negative images of themselves. Even if they are not overtly racist, the people who look after them may know little of the children's home backgrounds and fail to appreciate the importance of helping them to form a positive cultural identity. More recently the question of racial and cultural identity has become a matter of intense public debate in relation to placement. Indeed, under the Children Act 1989 it is now a factor that has to be taken into account when such decisions are made.

A consensus seems to have developed among social workers, supported by bodies such as British Agencies for Adoption and Fostering (BAAF), that black children who are fostered or adopted by white families will suffer from identity problems in adolescence and that they will be ill-equipped to cope with the racism that they are certain to encounter (Jervis, 1990). However it is important to note that Tizard and Phoenix in a comprehensive review of the American and British literature on the subject found no evidence for this view. Studies of black children adopted into white families as well as of mixed race children living with single white mothers have found no adverse effects on their self-esteem (Tizard and Phoenix, 1989). This research may offer some reassurance to social workers when the practical alternative to placing a black or mixed-race child with white foster carers is an unpredictably prolonged stay in a residential home where he or she will also usually be looked after by white staff, but without the personal commitment of adoptive or fostering arrangements. Much turns upon assumptions about the availability of carers of the same race as the children and thus upon the energy and resources which go into recruiting and supporting them.

There seems little doubt that the experience of leaving home to be looked after by a local authority may lead children to form negative images of themselves, whatever their colour. In the case of older children from ethnic minority families, this threat to their sense of identity may be compounded by dislocation from cultural origins and sometimes by unawareness or lack of understanding in their carers. Thus, children from ethnic minorities who come 'into care' may not only need their sense of cultural difference and worth to be preserved but in some cases actively promoted. The implications of this may be far-reaching, embracing questions of food, education, patterns of social and family relationships and attachments, expectations of independence and religious observance.

Social Presentation

There is an overwhelming body of evidence from social psychology that those who are considered to be physically attractive have many advantages in life. This is as true for children as it is for adults. Teachers, for example, are strongly influenced by physical appearance and tend to put attractive children in higher streams (Rist, 1973; Kenealy, 1988). Sociometric studies show that children choose friends at least partly on the basis of their appearance (Jackson, 1964; Dion and Bercheid, 1974). Friendships, in their turn, make a significant contribution to self-esteem. Children are liable to be stigmatised because of their unattractive appearance, unlikeable personal habits and inappropriate social behaviour (Nash, 1973). Given the other problems that children 'in care' have to face, they can ill-afford to be additionally burdened by handicaps like these.

However, studies of children leaving the care system suggest that insufficient attention is given to self-presentation and social skills. Youngsters often do not know how to deal effectively with adults, with their peers or with public situations and sometimes they cause unnecessary or unintended offence to others by their manner or, perhaps, by their lack of personal hygiene (Dickinson, 1988).

Some of the great advances of recent years in work to enable people with learning difficulties to live normal lives in the community have resulted from greater emphasis being placed upon self-presentation and public acceptability. The importance of these dimensions in relation to children for whom local authorities bear a responsibility has yet to be fully recognised. Yet ordinary parents do concern themselves with how their children are seen by others, even though they may find it difficult to modify certain aspects of the way their offspring conduct themselves. Again, what is crucial is not that parents should succeed in the endeavour but that they should try to set standards of which their children are aware even if they do not always choose to observe them.

III   Seeing the Whole Child

It might be argued that assessing outcomes along these seven separate dimensions produces a fragmented view. This is obviously not our intention. It is essential for the social worker to have a sense of the whole child, and we have already indicated some of the ways in which the different dimensions interact and overlap. The choice of several developmental dimensions as a basis for outcome assessment was informed by the need to have a detailed picture of the child's overall state, even though improvements along one dimension might have to be balanced against a lack of progress on others.

We have already discussed (in chapter 3) the case for and against attaching different weights to these different developmental areas and have explained why we decided against doing so. Nonetheless, it might be suggested that the dimensions have a changing significance in relation to each other for children of different ages; for instance, that education is more important at thirteen than at three, or that competence matters more at eighteen than at six. The contrary argument is that although certain dimensions emerge as significant at particular ages, outcomes at these ages depend to a large extent on the attention that they have received earlier. To assign differential values to the dimensions according to age would ignore this connection.

Of course, as we have argued earlier, social workers and others will always have to make practical choices between dimensions in setting their priorities; but if their attention is drawn to the nature of those choices they are more likely to do so after deliberate and careful consideration. In the process, unwarranted assumptions may be exposed or questions raised which would not otherwise have been asked.

We repeat that it is rarely possible to establish causal relationships in child care. There are too many uncontrollable factors, amongst which a child's experiences 'in care' may be of relatively minor significance. There are obvious dangers in being over-prescriptive: indicators can be misleading or culturally biased. They may easily become outdated. Nevertheless, every time social workers make statutory visits to foster homes, for example, they need to elicit certain information in order to fulfil their supervisory responsibilities. Often both the agenda and criteria for assessment on such occasions remain unstated and perhaps even below the level of consciousness; a formal system of assessment brings hidden judgements into the open.

There has been a tendency in the past for both social workers and researchers to assess outcome in an over-simplified way. Service outcomes have been measured solely in terms of making the requisite provisions and fulfilling the requirements of the law. Social workers are rarely held accountable for poor professional practice (Parker, 1990). At present it would be true to say that only a minimum of the tasks that most parents would undertake (or arrange for) without question are required of them. For example, there are few incentives for doing more than ensure that a child attends school and avoids trouble with the police. There are no compelling reasons to make efforts to maintain and seek out family contacts or to compensate for areas of difficulty. This is due, at least in part, to a lack of practical acknowledgement at both fieldwork and managerial levels that outcomes, by their very nature, are multi-dimensional. On the basis of research evidence and the experience of parents and practitioners, we have tried to show the importance for a child's current well-being and future life chances of each of the seven dimensions that we have selected: health; education; behavioural and emotional development; social and family relationships; identity; self-care and competence, and social presentation. We believe that this multi-dimensional approach will help social workers to monitor their own practice more effectively and assist managers to identify the gaps and weaknesses in the services that they offer to children for whom they carry some parental responsibility.

Outcome can never be predictable with any certainty and is likely to be the product of sequences of favourable or unfavourable events seldom attributable to any specific social work action or decision. However, although public authorities are not necessarily responsible for all the negative outcomes in the case of a particular child, they can be held accountable if they fail to ensure that all chidren in their care receive the type of experiences which are known from research evidence to be linked to success. In the next chapter we show how it is possible to specify what outcomes might reasonably be aimed for within each of the broad dimensions that have been discussed above. We can then go on to assess the extent to which these positive outcomes are achieved in reality.

Summary of Main Points from this Chapter

1. Social services departments give too much emphasis to assessing outcomes in terms of continuity of placement. Children may wait months or years for stable substitute homes, during which period active work might be undertaken to provide them with opportunities to achieve intermediate goals in other spheres. A multi-dimensional view of outcome is therefore needed.

2. The old poor law principle of less eligibility survives alongside the conflicting opinion that children who are looked after away from home should be given the same opportunities as those growing up in average families. The latter view should be promoted, in order to improve expectations for children looked after away from home, and to emphasise the local authority's role *in loco parentis*. The dimensions chosen should be applicable to all children, although they need to include areas that are particularly problematic for children looked after away from home.

3. The seven dimensions along which we recommend that outcomes should be assessed are introduced. The discussion on the dimension of *health* is used not only to examine which aspects of health care need to be monitored, but also to demonstrate certain other points that are relevant to the assessment in all the dimensions: these are that outcomes interact, so that poor health, for instance, affects a child's performance in other areas; that certain elements on any dimension

(in this case diet) will be culturally based, and need to be treated sensitively; and that a multi-dimensional approach mirrors the outlook of ordinary parents.

4. Important points from the discussion on the other dimensions are as follows:— *Education*, although of crucial importance to most parents, tends to be given a low priority when children are looked after by local authorities; poor achievements may be based on low expectations. Many children are looked after by local authorities because they have developed *emotional and behavioural difficulties* that cannot be contained at home. The continued presence or absence of such problems are important indicators of outcome. *Family and peer relationships* are areas in which children who live away from home are known to experience particular difficulty; links need to be fostered not only between the child and parents or parent substitutes, but also with other members of the extended family. All children need to develop *self-care skills*. Young people who are looked after away from home may be given complete independence at an age when their peers still expect to receive considerable emotional and practical support from parents and other relatives; they therefore need to develop a high level of competence in this area if they are to cope successfully. Children who are looked after away from home often develop a poor sense of *identity* and low self-esteem. Difficulties may be exacerbated when children from ethnic minorities are looked after by carers who have little understanding of their cultural background. Outcomes in this dimension should therefore be carefully scrutinised. Parents teach their children how to present themselves in such a way as to appear attractive to others. Other people's perceptions are particularly relevant to disadvantaged children who may encounter stigmatisation. Successful *social presentation* has beneficial repercussions in other developmental dimensions.

5. These dimensions are not weighted in order of importance: although some may appear more or less significant at certain ages, children need to develop continually along all these dimensions if they are to achieve long-term well-being in adulthood. This multi-dimensional method of assessing outcomes is intended to reflect the concerns of reasonable parents, who try to consider all relevant aspects of their children's development.

Chapter 7

The Monitoring Instrument

The preceding chapters have examined the complexity of the issues that surround the assessment of outcome and have mapped out an approach upon which a monitoring instrument might be based. In this chapter we explain the actual construction and use of such an instrument. The one we propose comprises a series of schedules adapted to children of different ages. Examples of these are included in Appendix 2, and should be referred to in conjunction with the discussion which follows.

Earlier versions of the schedules were piloted in four local authorities (Ward and Jackson, 1991) and in the light of the reactions of those who used them and of others whose views we sought, they have been modified and improved. The full range of schedules, covering all the age groups, is now available from HMSO together with guidelines for their use. An IBM-compatible computer programme is also available which enables the printed schedules to be dispensed with.

As we explained, the schedules seek to assess outcome by 'examining the extent to which those responsible for children have adopted parenting practices which are believed to influence the likelihood of success'. The Children Act 1989 sets as a standard of care that which a 'reasonable parent' would provide (sect.31; Department of Health, 1989a, p.6). The schedules give a detailed picture of what this might mean in practice. Thus they pose a range of simple questions designed to assess the extent and quality of the 'parental' inputs that each child receives. By inquiring about concrete parenting practices, they obviate the need to administer a complex barrage of tests and scales. Those responsible for children should be able to complete the forms without the assistance of other professionals. In this way, the schedules focus on the practices of ordinary parents, who rarely attempt to assess their children formally, but who are aware that certain actions are likely to produce desirable results. As we have pointed out, 'reasonable parents' try to ensure that their children will encounter the type of experiences that they regard as necessary to achieve a satisfactory outcome; but they do not expect to provide them all themselves.

The schedules are designed to assess outcome along each of the seven dimensions described in chapter 6. They were produced by first clarifying what the aims of a reasonable parent would be for children within specific age-groups along each dimension. These aims were then matched with a series of specific inputs that both research and common sense suggest are necessary for their achievement. Questions were then designed to elicit information about the parenting practices of those people responsible for a child's progress. Their replies should indicate the weak points of the service for a particular child; additional questions within each schedule are intended to enable those responsible to make further plans to improve 'parental' inputs, or to justify their deliberate omission.

The Children for Whom the Schedules are Designed

Chapter 5 recommended that outcome assessment should be applied to four groups of children: those in the care of local authorities; those accommodated by them; those living at home under supervision from social services departments, and those who experience separation through related services such as special education. Broadly speaking, these are the 'children in need' identified by the Children Act 1989.

The schedules are designed to be incorporated into the statutory review process, and therefore could most readily be used to assess children for whom local authorities have held particular responsibility for at least six months. Although it may not be considered necessary to evaluate the brief 'care' experiences of the large number of children who go home within a few days, about a third of them do in fact return, some on more than one occasion. At the very least therefore, social services departments should be encouraged to establish certain baseline data during the first episode of 'care' which would then provide a point of reference for making subsequent assessments if and when children were readmitted. Likewise, the schedules could well be applied to children who remain with their families under voluntary or statutory supervision, even though they are not subject to the reviewing requirements of the legislation. In these cases the schedules would be used in conjunction with interviews with parents or children during which those concerned could discuss what needed to be provided or done and share out unfulfilled tasks.

The Age of the Child

The assessment and action records can be used to assess outcomes for all children and young people, from birth to adulthood. The population for assessment has been divided into six age-groups: under 1, 1–2, 3–4, 5–9, 10–15 and 16 and over. These clusters correspond with certain developmental and social requirements that are expected of children at specific ages. Thus the shorter age-bands for the younger children reflect the extensive development that takes place between babyhood and school age. Babies and young children under three have been separated into two age-bands, the first cut-off point being where increased mobility allows for a rapid expansion of the infant's world, and the second being the age at which the child's experience begins to stretch beyond the immediate family. The next cluster ends where compulsory education begins: many of the intermediate outcomes that have been achieved by this age will determine the ease with which a child begins his or her school career. Nine marks an age at which intermediate outcomes may often indicate future difficulties for separated children; for example, there is some evidence to suggest that children who enter long-term foster placements in middle childhood are likely to find it difficult both to retain links with their natural families and to develop a compensatory relationship with substitutes (Millham *et al.*, 1986; Berridge and Cleaver, 1987). The next age-band, 10–15 years, was originally divided at thirteen. The first part covered the transition from junior to secondary school, and the second the years of puberty when offences by juveniles tend to peak, and when many children whose behaviour problems have previously been contained at home or in schools come to the notice of social services departments. However, on closer scrutiny it was decided that the aims and intermediate outcomes for these two age-groups were sufficiently similar to make a division unnecessary. A compromise was reached by producing one schedule to cover the whole age-group of 10–15 years old, but including one or two extra questions to be asked when the child reached thirteen. The next age-group begins at sixteen, the age at which many young people are preparing to leave school and embark upon employment. Until recently the 'parental' responsibilities assumed by local authorities ceased when young people reached their eighteenth birthdays; under the Children Act 1989, the duty to offer 'parental' advice and assistance has been extended until those who have formerly been cared for by the local authority reach the age of twenty-one (sect.24). For this reason, the last age-band is open-ended, since we do not yet know how this clause will be interpreted.

Thus, a series of six questionnaires has been designed in order to assess children within each of these age-groups. Although many of the recommended inputs remain constant throughout childhood, others alter as children develop and as 'parental' aims and expectations change.

Aims

Each section of the schedules concludes with questions concerning the outcomes that would generally be considered desirable within the specified age-ranges for each developmental dimension. As we have already suggested, although parents may have different aspirations for their children, there does appear to be a high degree of popular consensus about the general nature of their task. The aims set out in the schedules are intended to delineate such general expectations rather than to be rigidly prescriptive. They are, however, designed to indicate the views of the 'reasonable parent', and would seem to be relatively uncontentious. Nevertheless, how parents regard their tasks is influenced by their values; and the 'reasonable parent' is, of course, no more than a concept. Our values will inevitably have shaped our choice of aims. Indeed, with respect to these issues it is neither possible nor desirable for any of us to adopt an entirely objective stance.

The previous chapter described how, while considerations of less eligibility have long since ceased to be an overt part of local authority policy, aspirations for children in care remain disappointingly low. However, local authorities now have a duty to 'safeguard and promote the welfare of children within their area who are in need' and this should, in certain circumstances, oblige them to compensate for disadvantages in the child's background. The standard of public care will not be improved until expectations are increased, and, with this in mind, some recommended inputs have been deliberately set at a level that is as yet rarely attained. This is particularly true in the case of education, where we know that few children in care attend nursery school (Outcomes Working Party, 1988) or achieve average academic standards (Jackson, 1987).

The Questions in the Schedules about Inputs

The questions in the schedules about what has been done are all designed to discover whether the child is receiving (or has received) those parental-like inputs that are deemed necessary to achieve the aims specified at the conclusion of each of the seven dimensional sections.

Two of the major tasks of parenting are to build up a body of essential knowledge about a child, and to undertake certain actions which are perceived as necessary in order to attain desired outcomes. These two functions are interdependent, for no one can assess what more needs to be done without some understanding of a child's past history.

While birth parents may well acquire knowledge unconsciously simply by being present, social services departments have to take deliberate steps to ensure that certain facts about a child are collected, verified, and can be made available. For instance, whereas a parent may know if a child is allergic to penicillin because she can remember the incident which prompted the discovery, a corporate body needs to make specific inquiries and keep records in order to have this type of information available should it be needed. Certain items on the schedules are designed to build up this pool of detailed information about the child. It is not always necessary for social workers to verify information for themselves: administrative assistants might be asked to take on tasks such as checking birth certificates or liaising with health visitors in order to gather information about immunisations and infectious illnesses. However, it is the social worker's responsibility to ensure that the information is collected and adequately stored. A dossier of official documents, containing items such as a copy of a birth certificate and national health card, should be placed with the primary carer.

The schedules are designed to be filled in at regular intervals. It would be repetitive to ask those who complete them to record the same factual information every few months. Certain questions on the schedules are intended to remind social workers that such information needs to be collected; they are advised not to record it on the forms, but either on the child's case-paper or, preferably, on a 'basic fact sheet' devised specifically for that purpose and designed to align with the questions on the schedules. An example of such a sheet is reproduced in Appendix 3.

However, the majority of questions in the schedules are designed to produce a dynamic assessment of the quality of parenting offered to the child. Questions have been deliberately made as concrete as possible in an attempt to dissuade those who are making the assessment from an understandable tendency to skate over the surface of difficult issues rather than to confront them. Thus, for instance, respondents are required to ask the child to name his or her special friends and to state the frequency of contacts with relatives in order to provide evidence for themselves and others that desired outcomes are actively being sought, and not simply relegated to the realm of wishful thinking.

Although the majority of questions concerning inputs are directed at all children, a few will only be applicable to the older ones in each age group. While there may be some initial gaps, by the time a child reaches the top of each age range all questions in each category should be answerable.

It is probable that some of the proposed dimensions for assessment will assume greater prominence at certain ages, and less at others. For instance, the possession of a clear sense of identity appears much more crucial in adolescence than in early childhood. However, it is important to note that the assessment deals with developmental issues, all of which are gradual processes in the task of growing up: although emphases may change, no dimension can be overlooked with impunity at any age. It is possible that some of the questions on the competence dimension in particular may appear to be unduly prescriptive: however, the gradual acquisition of skills in dealing with the outside world is an aspect of development that has, in the past, often been overlooked for this group of children (Stein and Carey, 1986). The introduction of a detailed checklist of self-care skills that are appropriate for each age-group is intended to redress the balance.

Some of the recommended inputs are based on research findings; for instance, it is well known that children who attend pre-school facilities such as play groups and nursery schools are both socially and academically better able to make the transition to school than those who have spent their years entirely within their own families (Tizard et al., 1988). Others are based on common sense; for instance, if children do not look and smell well-cared for they are unlikely to win acceptance from unknown adults and peers. It must be stressed that, while desired outcomes are likely to remain relatively constant, the necessary inputs or routes by which they are achieved will change as social circumstances alter over time. The lists of questions will need to be checked and, if necessary, updated.

When a cohort of children receives all the recommended inputs, and results in the aggregate are unsatisfactory, the time will have come to question the connection between input and outcome.

Replying to the Questions

The task of completing each questionnaire is relatively time-consuming: however, it seems unlikely that an abbreviated version would provide sufficient insight into the quality of 'parenting' to produce an adequate assessment of outcome. On the other hand, because so much ground is covered, every effort has been made to produce a lay-out that is easy to follow. As far as possible open-ended questions have been avoided. The replies that have to be given are largely confined to single words that can be ticked off by the respondent, or scales that require a mark to be made along a continuum. These are readily quantifiable and, when aggregated, can provide important information about patterns of practice.

The number of positive replies to the questions in each schedule will provide some indication of the quality of care offered to each child. Negative replies do not necessarily indicate unsatisfactory care, but where children clearly require a greater level of input than they are receiving, either because of unintended omissions or through exceptional needs, respondents are required to formulate a plan for further action and decide who will carry it out.

Settling Responsibilities

When parents send a child to stay with a relative or friend, they only delegate a small part of their responsibility; they relinquish far more when their child is looked after by a local authority, in spite of the new legislation's attempt to encourage a sense of partnership between the parties involved. Even when children are simply accommodated by the authority, choices about school and placement may well be taken out of the parents' hands. When a care order is made, the local authority

113

acquires a wide range of parental responsibilities. Yet although parental powers can be invested in a local authority, their 'parental practices' are not always commensurate with standards found within the community. Thus in recent years research has shown that separated children may become isolated, and find it difficult to preserve a relationship with their parents (Millham *et al.*, 1986) or to develop strong links with substitutes (Berridge and Cleaver, 1987). They may also fail to establish close relationships with their peers (Tizard, 1988). They are likely to be educationally disadvantaged (Jackson, 1987). Perhaps most striking of all, they may leave 'care' without adequate preparation or a place in the community, at a time when most of their contemporaries would expect to receive parental support for a number of years (Stein and Carey, 1986).

Many of the shortfalls in practice arise through accidental omissions rather than through deliberate policy. Directors of social services are unlikely to meet the children for whom they are responsible but will delegate their care to a variety of people. Broadly speaking, the position of directors is analogous to that of High Court judges in wardship proceedings: while others are involved in the day-to-day care of the children, ultimate responsibility for each child's well-being rests with them. They may delegate the task of overall co-ordination and control to social workers, primary care to foster parents and, if rehabilitation is the aim, a range of specific tasks to families and perhaps to children as well. One reason why social work practice often appears to produce unsatisfactory results may be found in a confusion over this allocation of responsibility. One study recorded the case of a child who failed to sit an 'O' level because nobody regarded it as their job to make sure that she was at school on the day of the examination (Berridge, 1985). The schedules seek to ensure that this sort of confusion does not arise: the purpose of asking 'who will take further action?' is to clarify how essential 'parental' tasks are to be allocated between the different parties concerned in the child's welfare.

Where children are accommodated by a local authority the schedules should be used to enable social workers, natural parents and primary carers to decide how the task of parenting is to be divided: the result of such discussions could be used as a basis for the written arrangements required under the Regulations for the Arrangements for Placements of Children 1991. It is easy for parents to lose their confidence in performing simple everyday tasks for children from whom they have been separated. In the words of one parent to whom we spoke and who finally lost custody and access:

> Things like feeding and bathing. You grow accustomed to not doing it, and I think it is important that social workers should keep parents doing that sort of thing because otherwise they will end up feeling like I did, that they can't . . . Maybe if they'd kept me doing all those things all the way through and I'd had more frequent access, then I'd have felt a lot more ready at the time to have the children (Outcomes Working Party, 1988).

The allocation of some of these simple, practical tasks to parents might make successful rehabilitation a more realistic possibility in certain cases.

Parents who are planning to resume the care of their children should also be encouraged to undertake some of the necessary liaison with schools. For instance, foster carers could be asked to accompany birth parents to occasions which they might otherwise find daunting, such as school open days and interviews with teachers.

Even where there are no plans for immediate rehabilitation, a large proportion of children who are looked after by a local authority will eventually return to live with their parents. Our discussion with a group of birth parents revealed widespread concern at the lack of information which they received about their children while they were in care, an omission that is clearly detrimental to what may already be fragile relationships. Social services departments might well follow the example set by schools and furnish all parents who retain access with regular reports of the progress of children whom they look after. A proper use of the proposed schedules would provide ample information for such reports.

It is important to note that although it is the social worker's responsibility to ensure that parental functions are satisfactorily fulfilled, many of the necessary tasks can appropriately be delegated to others. Thus volunteers might be usefully employed in helping children to acquire appropriate self-care skills. Before making decisions with respect to children whom they are looking after, local authorities now have a duty under the new Act to 'ascertain the wishes and feelings . . . of the child, his parents, and any other person whose wishes and feelings they consider to be relevant' (sect.22). Thus the schedules assume that foster-carers, residential care officers, children and, in many cases, parents will be invited to participate in the review process and to undertake specific tasks. We recommend that foster carers play a greater part in making decisions and in planning than is often the case at present. Referrals to the child guidance service, for instance, come much more appropriately from primary carers who have a vested interest in querying delays than from social workers to whom problematic behaviour may be a less pressing concern.

The use of the schedules may also indicate a different kind of 'further action'; that is, the modification of practice or policies. For example, some of the necessary inputs on the education dimension, for school-age children in particular, require additional expenditure on items such as sports equipment, books or outings. It is possible that the replies in this section will demonstrate that children who are cared for by a local authority often miss out on these extra-curricular activities because, even when money is available, foster carers are reluctant to embark on the complicated process of claiming it. Local authorities could give foster carers and residential homes more autonomy by making available to them an allowance for educational extras, similar to the clothing allowance.

As children grow towards independence they need to take increasing responsibility for their own well-being. The schedules assume that, from the age of ten onwards, children will begin to undertake some of the 'parental' tasks themselves. For instance, if encouraged, even quite young children can take responsibility for eating fewer sweets, or for joining in extra-curricular activities that will broaden their interests. Indeed, many plans for future action will be unsuccessful unless children are willing to cooperate. Efforts to help children stop smoking, drinking alcohol or truanting from school will prove fruitless unless they, as well as the adults who are responsible for them, are willing to try to modify their behaviour. Lee (1981) has shown that formally involving children in plans for their care can prove extremely fruitful.

The schedules assume that, by the time young people reach sixteen, they will be taking at least some responsibility for many aspects of their lives. The form for assessing outcomes for older adolescents of sixteen and over is therefore designed to be filled in by the young people themselves, though social workers, foster carers, parents and others are expected to help them make and carry out plans where further action is required. Questions that might prove controversial, such as those that ask about the extent of young people's awareness of the dangers of alcoholism, smoking or unprotected sex, require them to state whether their social workers agree with their assessments. In order to ensure some degree of comparability, we recommend that the concluding questions in each section, which ask how far specific aims have been fulfilled, are completed by the social worker; there is, however, an opportunity for young people and carers to state where they disagree with these assessments.

Each schedule concludes with a summary, in which those who assess the quality of care a child receives are asked to record the plans that have been made for further action, the person to whom work has been delegated, and the target set for its completion.

Explanations for the Absence of Information or Action

Where a child is not receiving a necessary input and no further compensatory action is envisaged, the schedules call for an explanation to be given. Similarly, reasons are required for any decision not to pursue the quest for missing information.

Under the Poor Law the policy of less eligibility was used as a justification for many of the inadequacies of public child care.

Although the principles of the Poor Law have long since been officially abandoned, some negative responses to questions of why this or that is not being done may still be the result of local authority policies. For example, some authorities place limits on their parental role and clearly state that, in certain respects, they are unable to emulate the norms set by parents in the community (Outcomes Working Party, 1988). Others find their intentions frustrated by inadequate resources. All authorities are bound by certain restrictions which prevent them from offering separated children the same experiences that they might have hoped to receive from their families of origin. The cessation of care and concern when adulthood has been formally reached is an obvious instance where the statutory system falls short of common parental practice.

Notwithstanding these constraints, many authorities nowadays make every effort to compensate separated children for the disadvantages of their early experiences. In most respects these children are seen as requiring inputs that are identical to, or better than, those received by their contemporaries, but with one proviso: becuase of their special situation, there will be some circumstances in which it is necessary to place them under particular restrictions and to deny them certain rights in their own and other people's interests. Thus, some children 'in care' will be denied access to their parents on the grounds of their own physical safety or emotional stability. A restriction such as this will only be necessary for a minority: there is no reason why the great majority should not see their parents as much as they choose, and indeed, local authorities now have a duty to promote a child's contacts with relatives (Children Act 1989, sect.34). However, there is a danger that unless social workers are required to justify exceptional restrictions such as the withdrawal of access from particular children, these will come to be viewed as acceptable practices for the group as a whole.

Thus, a major purpose of the 'explanation for inaction' questions in the schedules is to oblige social workers to focus their attention on matters that might otherwise pass unnoticed, and to be held accountable for the things that they might reasonably be expected to do.

Measuring Well-being

The replies to the questions on the forms will indicate those areas where a child's progress is slow, or standards of care are poor. A second assessment will demonstrate how the situation has changed in the intervening months. Those who are concerned with the care of an individual child should therefore be able to measure progress without making a more precise analysis.

However, if an authority uses this method of assessment on a regular basis for a number of children, the data can be aggregated and analysed to provide information that should be useful to managers, policy makers and researchers about the overall strengths and weaknesses of services. The computer programme that accompanies this project has been designed to facilitate such an analysis. The data that lend themselves most readily to analysis are likely to be the replies to the 'aims' questions, the factual information that the schedules prompt social workers to record on files or basic fact sheets, and the explanations that are given for decisions not to act. These answers can all be scored and quantified. In the aggregate, replies to the 'aims' questions should indicate those areas of development in which groups of children are doing well, and those where outcomes are poor; it should therefore be possible to identify where improvements can be made to overall standards of care. The factual data should provide a local authority with information about such matters as the number of children under its care or supervision who are properly immunised, the frequency with which they change addresses and/or schools, and their success or failure in obtaining employment. The explanations can be quantified and used for several purposes. First, where omissions are the result of financial or legal restrictions, aggregate replies will demonstrate the extent of the acknowledged shortfall between local authority provisions and the parenting practices prevalent within the community. Secondly, where there is a professional decision not to secure a recommended input, explanations should provide valuable insights about the structure of the assumptions on which such exceptions are based.

* * *

The schedules will therefore generate data which have a variety of different applications: social workers can use them as a means of assessment and as a method of reviewing their own work, formulating future plans for a child and allocating various tasks to the many people whose roles combine to form the corporate parent. Managers can use the information to assess the overall quality of care being offered and to examine the effects of particular policies. The data will also provide a pool of quantifiable information which will be of considerable assistance to social work teachers and researchers.

The initial task of assembling detailed basic information about a child and assessing dynamic 'parental' inputs across a range of dimensions may seem to be a daunting undertaking, even though the number of questions to be answered about any particular child is not large. However, if adequate attention is given to the first review, subsequent assessments should not be complicated. Moreover, as suggested above, the task of gathering information can be shared among several participants. Above all, however, the use of our schedules will form an important part of the structure of local authorities' accountability for the children who come within the ambit of their services.

Summary of the Main Points from this Chapter

1. The schedules can be used to assess all children who are looked after or supervised by social services departments. They have been designed for incorporation into the statutory reveiw system, but can also be used to assess other children whom the local authority is not required to review, but for whom it acknowledges some responsibility.

2. The children to be assessed have been divided into six age-groups: under 1, 1–2, 3–4, 5–9, 10–15 and 16 and over. The divisions have been chosen to match developmental and social stages in children's lives.

3. Each section of the schedules concludes by asking how far a child has achieved a series of aims that are related to his or her age and the developmental dimension being assessed. Preceding questions are designed to discover whether the child is receiving those parental inputs that both research and common sense would suggest are necessary to the achievement of these aims. Although the aims are likely to remain constant, the recommended inputs will alter in the light of further research findings and changing social circumstances.

4. The schedules need to be completed by all those responsible for the care of a child, in consultation. Parents and older children should be encouraged to play a part in the assessment and subsequent decision-making.

5. Where gaps are noted in the care a child receives, those responsible are required to formulate a plan for further action and decide who will carry it out. Respondents are required to explain any decisions not to take particular actions for individual children.

6. The data gathered through using the schedules can be scored and analysed. When aggregated, the replies to the questions on aims, the explanations for decisions not to act and the factual information that social workers are prompted to record, should provide information of use to planners, managers, policy-makers and researchers.

Chapter 8

From Assessment to Action: Results from the Pilot Study

The type of assessment described in the previous chapter is far more detailed than the methods used at present by most local authorities. It also covers a wider range of developmental dimensions than those usually considered. Before making the schedules generally available, it was therefore important to pilot them in order to find out whether they would fulfil the several functions for which they had been designed. In particular we wanted to know whether they could produce useful information, what effect they would have on social work practice, and whether, as intended, they could generate a sense of partnership between the various people who are responsible for outcome. Above all, we wanted to know whether regular use of the schedules could improve outcomes for children and young people 'in care'. This stage of the pilot study has now been completed.

Description of the Study

Five local authorities took part in this stage of the pilot study, which was designed to assess the feasibility of the schedules for use with children in two age-ranges, 3–4 years and 16–18 years. In four authorities, twelve field social workers were each asked to complete the schedules for one child on their caseload. Designated children had to have been under the care or formal supervision of the local authority for at least six months. The children were assessed on two occasions, separated by a three months interval. The researchers met the social workers at the start of the study, and after each completion of the schedules, when they were also asked to fill in a short checklist. The following paragraphs give a brief description of the findings of the pilot study. A fuller analysis can be found elsewhere (Ward and Jackson, 1991; Ward, Jackson and Parker, 1991). In the fifth authority, the schedules were used to assess the quality of care received by teenagers in two community homes with education. It was the responsibility of residential staff to ensure that they were completed. The results from this authority are not readily comparable with those from the others and have not been included in the following discussion.

Thirty-two social workers from the first four authorities participated in the study; thirteen used the schedule designed for 3–4 year olds, and nineteen that for 16–18 year olds. Nineteen social workers completed both assessments; thirteen others made one assessment, but were unable to complete the project, due to constraints on time.

It should be noted that the results described below come from a small sample of social workers who volunteered to participate in what was, essentially, a research exercise. In the second stage of the pilot study, which is due to begin at the time this book is published, the schedules will be introduced as agency policy for statutory reviews among a cross section of social workers. Amongst other things, results from that study will be used to confirm or refute some of the more tentative evidence described below.

Will the Schedules be Acceptable to Those Who are Asked to Complete Them?

Social workers were asked to look critically at the schedules and give us their opinions on such issues as their design, clarity and usefulness. Most appear to have found them easy to use, and a number of their comments were extremely enthusiastic. One wrote: '[the] young person enjoyed completing [the] questionnaire and it was a very useful tool for bringing up a whole range of issues from the very practical (needing to arrange visits to the dentist/optician) to the very complex and emotional'; another said that 'it's about focusing the care plans, about what needs to be achieved with individuals.'

Some social workers were initially concerned that foster carers would feel threatened by an exercise which could be used to criticise their work. These fears proved unjustified. Foster carers who completed a second assessment welcomed the proof it gave of change in the child's situation; they could see that progress had been made during the three months period between assessments. Social workers found that using the forms made it easier to introduce delicate topics, such as the possible permanence of the placement, which they had previously avoided for fear of upsetting foster carers. One social worker wrote that it was 'a useful way of sharing a discussion about a child with foster parents giving them a good, interesting way of assessing a child's progress and their part in it'. The usefulness of the schedules in training foster carers will be one of the issues examined in the next stage of the research.

We do not at present have detailed information about how parents and children viewed the exercise. The possible value of the schedules in involving them more closely in decision-making is discussed later in this chapter. A small number of adolescents refused to participate in the project. We do not know whether this was due to their genuine reluctance to undertake what may have seemed a daunting exercise, a general disenchantment with the care service or perhaps the way in which the project was presented to them. Reluctance to participate, and the ethical considerations this raises in connection with statutory work, are other issues to be addressed in the second phase of the planned research. The revised schedule for young people of sixteen years and over has been redesigned in such a way as to make the exercise more attractive to them.

The majority of criticisms received concerned specific issues in the design and layout of the forms, rather than their conceptual basis. These comments were extremely useful to the researchers, and were taken into account in revising the schedules, prior to publication. Representatives from Black and in Care, the Family Rights Group, the National Foster Care Association, and groups of young people in care and their parents were asked to comment on the schedules. Their replies have also contributed to the final design.

On the basis of our research, we believe that the most appropriate use of the schedules will be in preparing for statutory reviews. As chapter 1 has explained, research into current arrangements for reviews of children's cases shows them to be frequently perfunctory (Sinclair, 1984; Gardner, 1985). The Children Act 1989 introduces new and more stringent regulations which are aimed at raising the quality of reviews, and the schedules have been designed to align with their requirements (Department of Health, 1991). The forms are intended to be used at an initial review, to set a base-line standard of care, and subsequently, at either six-monthly or annual intervals, to monitor the extent to which the everyday tasks of parenting are being carried out. The recommendations for future work, made after completing one of the schedules, can provide the basis for making formal plans about a child, also required under the new legislation. The plan should also include overall arrangements not covered by the schedules, such as the purpose of the care episode, its expected duration, arrangements for access, and the suitability of the placement. We have developed formats both for making initial plans and for reviewing children which meet the requirements of the new regulations, and which tie in with the schedules. These were compiled after examining procedures in the five authorities participating in the pilot study. Examples are enclosed in the appendix to this book. The plans, the review forms, the basic facts sheets (described in chapter 7) and the schedules combine to form a complete package for planning, monitoring and assessing the care provided by a local authority to the children for whom it takes responsibility.

Only one social worker was definitely opposed to her authority adopting the schedules as agency policy. Of the others, those who had reservations about making such a recommendation generally objected to the length of time the work would take. Various steps have been taken to reduce the length of the schedules, but it remains an inescapable fact that this type of assessment, which has been designed to ensure a high standard of everyday care for all children looked after by a local authority, takes time and effort to complete. If the new regulations for reviews are to be met, social workers will, in any case, need to devote more time to monitoring children's development.

Will the Schedules Produce Useful Information?

Although our sample of completed schedules is too small to form a basis for any but tentative conclusions, nevertheless, their content does demonstrate the type of information that they are capable of engendering, and the ways in which it might be used.

It was encouraging to discover that some children were apparently receiving a higher standard of care than previously reported research had led us to expect. For example, those caring for 3–4 year olds were asked whether the child in question attended a nursery or playgroup at least once a week specifically because it has been suggested that young children in care are rarely offered the opportunity of pre-school education or of mixing with their peers (Outcomes Working Party, 1988). However, all eight children in this age-group for whom schedules were returned had been given this experience. Another interesting piece of evidence concerns the educational qualifications of the adolescents in the sample. Research suggests that the education of children who are cared for by local authorities is widely neglected (Kahan, 1979; Jackson, 1987; Fletcher-Campbell and Hall, 1990). We had expected that a record of the qualifications gained by young people in the study would reflect these findings, but this proved over-pessimistic. GCSE results had been obtained by eleven adolescents in the sample: four of them had five or more passes, one had three, and one one pass. It should, however, be noted that only two of the students achieved the higher grades (A-C). Two of the five young people who had reached school leaving age with no qualifications had special needs and were remaining in full-time education. However, three young people were embarking on their working lives with no qualifications, and two others had failed to ascertain their GCSE results several months after they had been announced.

It should be noted that these results are based on a very small sample of hand-picked children, and it is possible that social workers chose their more promising cases for scrutiny. As has already been mentioned, a number of adolescents refused to take part in the study, for reasons that remain unclear; this group might well have proved less successful than those who participated. Nevertheless, it is gratifying to find that the schedules indicated strengths, as well as weaknesses, in local authority services for children. At a time when the actions of social workers come under increasing public criticism, local authorities need to be able to establish that their services can be effective. The schedules can be used to provide such information.

On the other hand, much of the evidence from the piloted schedules does give cause for concern. Two thirds of the younger children had experienced more than one change of carer. Three quarters of the adolescent group were regular smokers. Only two of the ten who were not in school or further education were in full-time regular work.

Although the figures are too small to establish their significance, there also appeared to be a distinct tendency for the more successful young people to have plans to remain with natural or foster families after leaving care. All but one of the young people who went on to further education, and both those who had found full-time, regular work after leaving school, planned to remain with relatives, parents or foster carers after the local authority withdrew from the scene. On the other hand, those who had no qualifications and no regular occupation were also more likely to have little family support, and to find themselves at eighteen or younger, living on state benefits in lodgings, single bedsits, or flats shared with other young people. It is possible that both the failure of family support and the paucity of employment prospects were related to unacceptable behaviour displayed by these young people; nevertheless, the finding is in line with recent research which shows that those who are least able to cope tend to leave care with the least support (Bonnerjea, 1990).

This point should be given particular consideration, for it is indicative of a thorny problem: although local authorities need to prepare young people for independent living, they are at the same time required to offer continuing support to the immature. It is all too easy to justify failure or inadequacies of care by citing the young person's growing need for independence. The schedules were designed to require social workers to justify the omission of recommended actions. Many explanations appeared perfectly reasonable; others seem more doubtful. At sixteen or seventeen several adolescents in the sample were considered old enough to make up their own minds about issues such as smoking, exercise and diet; it was often left entirely to them to contact doctors, dentists, and sometimes schools for undiscovered GCSE results.

We do not know at what age the young people were considered to have reached this state of maturity, for younger adolescents were not assessed in this exercise; nor do we have much information about the length of time that parents expect to provide support and guidance for young people in the community. Recent research has, however, indicated that independence is often thrust upon young people 'in care' when they reach late adolescence, regardless of their readiness to cope alone (Stein and Carey, 1986); it seems possible that social workers' assessments of the level of maturity reached by some of the young people in the sample were similarly unrealistic.

A related problem was revealed in the completed schedule for younger children. In reply to the questions: 'Has the child been told why s/he is not living with own parents?' and 'Has an up-to-date life-story book been made and discussed with the child?', the child's immaturity or previous vicissitudes were often invoked as a reason for lack of action. It is hard to tell how far such claims can be justified, how far they are derived from a limited knowledge of child development, or whether they simply conceal an understandable reluctance to tackle difficult issues.

If the schedules are formally adopted by an authority, supervisors could gain much by considering the validity of the reasons given for omitting recommended tasks. In a number of instances, no reasons were given, and an analysis of these unexplained anomalies could prove to be equally revealing.

Indeed, the replies revealed a number of surprising omissions: for instance, at least 4 out of the 16 adolescents had reached the age of sixteen or more without receiving any information from adults about sexually transmitted diseases and contraception. Perhaps less unexpected was the discovery that 10 out of 23 (43%) children and adolescents had not seen a dentist since their last review. Although such a finding provides only a very crude indication of the quality of dental care (for the question was not worded in such a way as to discover how many children failed to make regular six-monthly visits), only one social worker who answered in the negative stated that an appointment had been arranged for a future date.

In many instances social workers were able to pick up such practical points from the use of the schedules, and deal with them immediately: arrangements were hastily made to provide counselling for those young people who were unaware of the dangers of AIDS and the importance of using contraceptives. Dental appointments were planned for seven of the ten children whose teeth had not recently been inspected, and at least four of these had been carried out within three months of the first assessment. Thus it seems probable that a scheme such as the one proposed, which evaluates the quality of care on a regular basis, can serve to heighten awareness of omissions, and bring about immediate improvements in practice.

What Effect do the Schedules have on Practice?

Social workers were asked whether participation in the research had enabled them to think more clearly about any of the seven dimensions of development covered by the schedules. The majority of the respondents thought that this had been either definitely or possibly the case in every dimension; 75% said that their awareness of health issues and 60% their awareness of a child's need to develop self-care skills and establish a sense of identity had definitely increased. Only one social worker among the 25 respondents said that there had been no change in her thinking on any dimension.

One of the few adverse comments on the pilot study came from a residential worker who wrote: 'I am unable to see that the case monitoring records would be of use to experienced child care staff caring for adolescents, either for reviews or for general use. They only repeat what we already have on file and know about our young people'. If this were generally the case, then the introduction of a complex method of assessment such as the one which we propose would be redundant. Sadly, many research studies have shown that such a state of affairs is by no means universally achieved. We have already observed, in chapter 7, that when responsibility for a child is divided among a number of people there is always a risk that necessary actions will be overlooked. Indeed, most of the shortfalls in public care occur through default rather then deliberate intention (DHSS, 1985). The schedules attempt to address this problem by requiring those involved in the care of a child to decide between themselves who will undertake each necessary 'parental' action and to record how the responsibilities have been divided. The requirement that decisions should be taken jointly is intended to improve practice by fostering communication between social workers, residential staff, foster carers, parents and children themselves.

The child care service as we know it today has evolved from the provisions made both by the poor law authorities and the voluntary societies in the late nineteenth century. Ward (1990) has demonstrated the persistence of historical traditions in contemporary social work. One of the most persistent assumptions from the nineteenth century, that arose from the rigid class system of the time, was the belief that there was little point in consulting the opinions of clients, for those in authority, who came from a superior social class would, *ipso facto*, know what was best for them. Apart from a few autobiographical accounts, the views of social work clients were unrecorded and unregarded until Mayer and Timms published their work in 1970.

Both this and later studies (see Fisher *et al.*, 1986) have drawn attention to the ease with which misunderstandings can arise if social workers fail to grasp that their clients may have different objectives, and alternative points of view.

It is also well recognised that foster carers and to some extent residential workers are often excluded when vital decisions are made about children (Sinclair, 1984). One of the most positive features of the Children Act 1989 is the stress that it places upon the development of a sense of partnership between those who are involved in the care of a child. The establishment of official complaints procedures emphasises that the views of parents, children and foster carers must now be taken into consideration (sect. 26). If a partnership between primary carers, children, parents and social workers is to exist in more than just name then all relevant parties must be invited to take a share in decision-making.

With this in mind, the schedules were designed to ensure that primary carers and the children themselves would have a voice in the assessment of their progress. This aim would appear largely to have been met. Twenty-three (77%) parents, foster parents and residential workers participated in the first assessments, as did fifteen (83%) of the older children. In the seven cases where no specific primary carer had apparently been consulted, four social workers had been aided by unspecified 'others', and the remaining three had completed the form with the co-operation of the young person (16–18 year old) alone. No social workers completed the first assessment without the involvement of at least one other interested party. All but five social workers said that completing the schedules had encouraged them to include other interested parties more fully in decision-making. Three of the dissenters claimed that there was no increased participation because they already gave a high priority to including all the relevant people.

The evidence that the use of the schedules fosters a sense of partnership between the various people who are involved in the care of the child is supported by some of the participants' comments. For example, a sixteen year old boy thought it 'great fun' and his social worker said that it had prompted more real conversation between them than she had achieved in all their previous encounters.

Will the Regular Use of the Schedules Improve Outcomes for Children and Young People 'in Care'?

There seems good reason to expect that regular use of the schedules will improve social work practice both in raising consciousness about a number of issues that are crucial to a child's development and in encouraging communication between all the parties, including parents and children, who are responsible for outcome. However, the crucial question is whether improved practice will improve outcomes. A final look at the type of changes that will be necessary to ensure that children who are the responsibility of local authorities are offered the opportunities to achieve long-term well-being in adulthood might shed further light on the matter.

So far, the published views of those who have spent their childhoods 'in care' have been hardly encouraging. Few have recounted experiences that match the abuses described by Graham Gaskin or Noele Arden (MacVeigh, 1982; Arden, 1977); nevertheless, most accounts dwell on the drawbacks rather than the benefits that resulted from admission (Page and Clark, 1977; see also Triseliotis and Russell, 1984). It is, of course, quite possible that it is mainly those whose experience of 'care' has been unfortunate who feel motivated to write about it. Triseliotis found that the majority of a group of young people who had grown up in foster care had positive experiences to relate (1980). Research being undertaken at present with a group of young people who spent periods of their childhood in 'care' but feel themselves to be successful as adults may serve to redress the balance further in the future (Jackson, 1991).

One can argue that the unsatisfactory nature of children's perceptions of care are only to be expected. Many of those who are separated from their parents labour under the type of overwhelming difficulties that are bound to colour their memories of childhood: desertion, sexual abuse or rejection, for instance, all leave scars that are difficult, if not impossible to eradicate. However, reported accounts from those who have been 'in care' do not criticise the inability of social workers to solve the intractable problems of the past so much as their refusal to address the difficulties of the present. Page and Clark suggest that:

> Perhaps professional workers have tended to pay too little attention to the day-to-day experiences of the child in the residential home, in school, in the neighbourhood, and ultimately at work because their adult perceptions lead them to concentrate upon the significance of what happened to the child in the past. For the child, time is now. Our group expressed a common complaint: 'They (residential and field social workers) keep going on about what happened years ago' (Page and Clark, 1977, p. 18).

Festinger (1983) invited a group of young American adults who had been 'in care' to name the issues on which agencies should focus in preparing adolescents for discharge. Those areas in which they felt their own preparation had been inadequate were: money management, further education, medical care, household living tasks, and counselling on growing up, marriage and parenting. Young people who have been brought up 'in care' in Britain raise similar issues. Many consider that they have lost out on their childhood, without ever having had the opportunity to grow up (Kahan, 1979).

It is, of course, extremely difficult for social workers, who are required to cope with regular crises, to devote attention to the apparently insignificant tasks that are necessary if children are to have the experiences that reasonable parents might be expected to provide. Checking that a baby has, for instance, been given the recommended immunisations must seem of very minor importance if she has previously been at risk of serious abuse. Nevertheless, removing a child from a damaging environment does not absolve those responsible for his or her long-term well-being from ensuring that the more humble, minor requirements for the achievement of satisfactory outcomes are remembered.

More than anything else the schedules have been designed to address this situation. By making explicit the simple, everyday tasks that must be completed if satisfactory outcomes are to be achieved, the schedules point those responsible to the small, practical steps which they can take to improve the quality of life for children whose other difficulties may prove impossible to remedy. As we have noted earlier, there is no guarantee of success, for although these actions are necessary, they will not always be sufficient to ensure satisfactory outcomes for all children. Nevertheless, if enough of them are taken, and enough opportunities offered and grasped, there is a chance that for some children, the earlier damage may be repaired (Rutter et al., 1983).

Summary of Main Points from this Chapter

1. Results from the pilot study are based on the opinions of 32 social workers in four local authorities, each of whom used the schedules to assess outcomes for one child on their case-load on two occasions, separated by a three months interval.

2. The majority of social workers found the schedules acceptable, and a number were extremely enthusiastic. The main criticism concerned their length. Opinions of other participants are not known at this stage.

3. The exercise indicated strengths as well as weaknesses in the child care service. More children attended nursery school, and more teenagers had academic qualifications than had been expected.

4. On the other hand 75% of teenagers smoked, and only 20% of those who were not in school or full-time education were in full-time regular work. There was a tendency for the more successful young people to have plans to remain with natural or foster families after leaving care, while those with the fewest resources were the most likely to be discharged to single, unsupervised accommodation. A surprising

number of adolescents had reached sixteen without receiving any information from adults about sexually transmitted diseases and contraception. Dental care appeared to have been often neglected.

5. Most social workers thought that using the schedules had helped them to think more clearly about children's development across the seven dimensions. They also felt that they had been encouraged to include other interested parties more fully in decision-making.

6. The schedules appear to have the potential to improve practice. Many of the omissions discovered at the first assessment had been rectified by the second. We do not yet know whether improved practice will improve outcome. The published views of those who have spent their lives 'in care' complain that too much attention was given to their past circumstances and too little to their needs of the present. It is to be hoped that, by setting out the simple practical tasks that parents undertake with the aim of ensuring positive outcomes for their children, the schedules will help those responsible to see how they can improve the quality of life of children whose other difficulties may prove impossible to remedy.

Conclusion

The rationale for allowing the State to intervene in the private sphere of family life has always been that either children, adults or the wider society will benefit by the intrusion. A hundred years ago, the benefits of providing separate care for deprived and disadvantaged children were thought to be self-evident. It has since become increasingly apparent that unless outcomes in child care can be adequately measured, we have no means of justifying the actions of social workers, which may have far-reaching and permanent consequences for individuals.

The extreme complexity of the issues involved in assessing outcomes is demonstrated by the fact that it has taken the working party, meeting at admittedly irregular intervals, four years to produce a scheme and to test its feasibility. Even now, further research is required before the tentative findings described in chapter 8 can be confirmed.

The system which we propose measures outcomes from the point of view of the individual child, and asks how far the experience of being looked after or supervised by a local authority has enhanced his or her chances of achieving long-term well-being in adulthood. The system does not rely on the administration of a complex barrage of tests and scales. Reliable psychometric tests have not yet been devised for several of the areas of development that we thought it necessary to measure. Nor would it be realistic to expect social workers to elicit and interpret the vast quantity of information that would be required to place a child's overall progress accurately on a mathematical scale. Moreover, it would not be possible to tell whether changes in position were related to the quality of care provided or to extraneous factors such as the child's experiences at school or the natural processes of maturation. Those who provide care are not in control of all the factors which determine outcome, and therefore cannot be held responsible for each individual success or failure.

Therefore our system does not attempt to determine the point that a child has reached on a developmental continuum. Instead, it takes as its starting point the State's acquisition of parental rights and responsibilities. It sets out a number of aims that a reasonable parent might be expected to hold for children across a range of ages and developmental dimensions and asks whether children looked after or supervised by local authorities are receiving the type of experiences that are requisite to their achievement. Thus it concentrates on the areas over which local authorities have some control, and for which they may be held accountable.

In part, this is a straightforward system of measurement, designed to be applicable to all children in need. However the value to be gained from assessing the outcomes of child care can be greatly enhanced if the task carries within it the potential for redressing anomalies and rectifying omissions. Thus the system we propose not only measures outcomes, but also encourages those who use it to make and record plans for their improvement. Preliminary results suggest that the task of assessment itself can raise consciousness about areas of children's development which have previously been overlooked, and thereby improve practice. The system is also designed to ensure that proposed partnerships between foster carers, social workers, children and birth families become a reality.

One of the key functions of the reasonable parent is to provide continuity in the life of a child. The early child care services were developed from a contradictory assumption: that the purpose of social work with children was to provide not continuity, but a clean break with the past. This assumption has increasingly been questioned, but never entirely eradicated. Recent research shows that the lives of children who are looked after by a local authority may be characterised by a string of further discontinuities and disruptions (see for instance Millham *et al.*, 1986; Berridge and Cleaver, 1987). It is hoped that this system of assessment will ensure some form of continuity in the quality of care provided to children looked after away from home. Perhaps its greatest advantage will be its ability to break down the complicated task of bringing up a child into a series of practical steps that can be undertaken at the appropriate times by whoever is acting as the primary carer, and regardless of other complications that may arise. Such an approach emphasises that outcomes in child care involve more than the resolution of placement difficulties, and enables active work to continue at all times.

Appendix One

List of those who attended the first meeting on assessing outcomes in child care, held at Dartington Hall, Devon, April 1987.

Dr Jane Aldgate	Department of Applied Social Studies and Social Research, University of Oxford
Dr David Berridge	National Children's Bureau
Mr Roger Bullock	Dartington Social Research Unit University of Bristol
Ms Hedi Cleaver	Dartington Social Research Unit University of Bristol
Dr Carolyn Davies	Research Management Division Department of Health
Mr Kenneth Hosie	Dartington Social Research Unit University of Bristol
Mr Rupert Hughes	Community Services Division Department of Health
Ms Sonia Jackson	Department of Social Work University of Bristol
Professor Martin Knapp	Personal Social Services Research Unit, University of Kent

Dr Michael Little	Dartington Social Research Unit University of Bristol
Mr Peter McCoy	Social Services Department Suffolk County Council
Professor Spencer Millham	Dartington Social Research Unit University of Bristol
Dr Jean Packman	Department of Social Work University of Exeter
Professor Roy Parker (Chairperson)	Department of Social Policy and Social Planning, University of Bristol
Mr Michael Power	Department of Social Policy and Social Planning, University of Bristol
Ms Wendy Rose	Social Services Inspectorate Department of Health
Ms Jane Rowe, OBE	British Agencies for Adoption and Fostering
Professor Barbara Tizard	Thomas Coram Research Unit Institute of Education University of London
Dr June Thoburn	Social Work Development Unit University of East Anglia
Professor John Triseliotis	Department of Social Policy and Social Work, University of Edinburgh
Dr Harriet Ward (Academic Secretary)	Department of Social Policy and Social Planning, University of Bristol
Professor Peter Wedge	Social Work Development Unit University of East Anglia
Professor Dorothy Whitaker	Department of Social Work University of York

Appendix Two

<table>
<tr><td>**H**</td><td>**Health**</td><td style="text-align:right">5–9 years</td></tr>
</table>

The questions in this section are designed to make sure that all preventive health measures have been taken, that all health problems/disabilities are being treated, that the child is adequately protected against common accidents and that, as far as possible, s/he is normally well.

H 1 Has the child had a medical examination since admission/last review? (*see guidelines*)

☐ Yes   ☐ No   ☐ Don't know

What recommendations were made?

Have all these been carried out?

☐ Yes   ☐ No   ☐ Don't know
☐ Not applicable: no recommendations

Who will take further action if necessary?

☐ Parent   ☐ Social Worker   ☐ Foster Carer
☐ Residential Worker   ☐ Other   ☐ No action needed

Explanation for lack of information or no action.

H 2 What is the child's height?

☐☐☐ cms   ☐☐☐ centile

What is the child's weight?

☐☐☐ kg   ☐☐☐ centile

Date when measured

☐☐☐☐☐☐

Is growth within normal limits? (*see guidelines*)

☐ Yes   ☐ No   ☐ Don't know

If not has s/he been referred for advice and/or treatment?

☐ Yes   ☐ No   ☐ Don't know
☐ Not applicable

What further action is needed?

Question **H 2** continues overleaf

Question **H 2** continues

Who will take it?

☐ Parent ☐ Social Worker ☐ Foster Carer

☐ Residential Worker ☐ Other ☐ No action needed

Explanation for lack of information or no action

H 3 Did the child receive the pre-school booster immunisation?

☐ Yes ☐ No ☐ Don't know

Has this been recorded?

☐ Yes ☐ No ☐ Don't know

Who will take further action if necessary?

☐ Parent ☐ Social Worker ☐ Foster Carer

☐ Residential Worker ☐ Other ☐ No action needed

Explanation for lack of information or no action

H 4 Has the child been prescribed glasses?

☐ Yes ☐ No ☐ Don't know

Does s/he wear them?

☐ Yes ☐ No ☐ Don't know

Has the child been prescribed a hearing aid?

☐ Yes ☐ No ☐ Don't know

Does s/he wear it?

☐ Yes ☐ No ☐ Don't know

Have any visual and/or hearing abnormalities been noted since the last review?

☐ Yes ☐ No ☐ Don't know

If yes, have these been recorded?

☐ Yes ☐ No ☐ Don't know

☐ Not applicable

What further action is needed?

Who will take it?

☐ Parent ☐ Social Worker ☐ Foster Carer

☐ Residential Worker ☐ Other ☐ No action needed

Explanation for lack of information or no action

H5 Has the child visited a dentist in the last six months?

☐ Yes ☐ No ☐ Don't know

What recommendations were made?

☐ Extractions ☐ Fillings ☐ Inspection, no treatment

☐ Other ☐ Not applicable

Have all these been carried out?

☐ Yes ☐ No ☐ Don't know

☐ Not applicable

Who will take further action if necessary?

☐ Parent ☐ Social Worker ☐ Foster Carer

☐ Residential Worker ☐ Other ☐ No action needed

Explanation for lack of information or no action

H 6 Is the child receiving necessary treatment for all chronic or recurrent medical conditions (e.g. asthma/glue ear)?

☐ Yes ☐ No ☐ Don't know

☐ Not applicable

Have all these been recorded?

☐ Yes ☐ No ☐ Don't know

☐ Not applicable

What further action is needed?

Who will take it?

☐ Parent ☐ Social Worker ☐ Foster Carer

☐ Residential Worker ☐ Other ☐ No action needed

Explanation for lack of information or no action

H 7 Are all physical problems (e.g. squint) being dealt with?

☐ Yes ☐ No ☐ Don't know

☐ Not applicable

What further action is needed?

Who will take it?

☐ Parent ☐ Social Worker ☐ Foster Carer

☐ Residential Worker ☐ Other ☐ No action needed

Explanation for lack of information or no action

143

H 8 Has the child had any other illnesses
since the last review?   ☐ Yes   ☐ No   ☐ Don't know

If yes, what were they?

Have all significant illnesses been
recorded?   ☐ Yes   ☐ No   ☐ Don't know

☐ Not applicable

What further action is needed?

Who will take it?

☐ Parent   ☐ Social Worker   ☐ Foster Carer

☐ Residential Worker   ☐ Other   ☐ No action needed

Explanation for lack of information or no action

H 9 Has the child attended hospital since
the last review?   ☐ Yes   ☐ No   ☐ Don't know

If yes, why?

Have all overnight stays in hospital
been recorded?   ☐ Yes   ☐ No   ☐ Don't know

☐ Not applicable

What further action is needed?

Who will take it?

☐ Parent   ☐ Social Worker   ☐ Foster Carer

☐ Residential Worker   ☐ Other   ☐ No action needed

Explanation for lack of information or no action

144

H 10 How often does the child eat or drink the following?

	Daily	Once a week or more	Less than once a week	Don't know
Fresh fruit	☐	☐	☐	☐
Fresh or frozen vegetables	☐	☐	☐	☐
Rice/Pasta/Wholemeal bread	☐	☐	☐	☐
Fresh meat/Fish/Eggs/Cheese	☐	☐	☐	☐
Half pint of milk	☐	☐	☐	☐
Sweets/Fizzy drinks	☐	☐	☐	☐
Chips	☐	☐	☐	☐

Do you consider that this is a satisfactory diet?

☐ Yes   ☐ Doubtful   ☐ No

☐ Don't know

If unsatisfactory, what further action will be taken?

Who will take it?

☐ Parent   ☐ Social Worker   ☐ Foster Carer

☐ Residential Worker   ☐ Other   ☐ No action needed

Explanation for lack of information or no action

H 11 Does the child have daily opportunities for vigorous physical activity?

☐ Yes   ☐ No   ☐ Don't know

If no or don't know, what further action will be taken?

Who will take it?

☐ Parent   ☐ Social Worker   ☐ Foster Carer

☐ Residential Worker   ☐ Other   ☐ No action needed

Explanation for lack of information or no action

145

H 12 Has the child's carer taken steps to ensure that:

All medicines, cleaning fluids and poisonous substances are kept out of reach?

☐ Yes ☐ No ☐ Don't know

Fires are adequately protected with guards?

☐ Yes ☐ No ☐ Don't know

The child learns and uses the Road Safety Code?

☐ Yes ☐ No ☐ Don't know

Who will take further action if necessary?

☐ Parent ☐ Social Worker ☐ Foster Carer

☐ Residential Worker ☐ Other ☐ No action needed

Explanation for lack of information or no action

HAVE THE FOLLOWING AIMS BEEN ACHIEVED?

AH 1 The child is normally well and thriving in growth and development

Frequently ill and/or failing to thrive |———————————| Normally well and thriving

---

AH 2 All preventive health measures, including appropriate immunisations, have been taken

Not enough attention to prevention |———————————| All preventive health measures have been taken

---

AH 3 All health problems/disabilities are being adequately treated

Not sufficiently treated |———————————| Adequately treated

☐ No problems

AH 4 The child is reasonably protected against common accidents

Several hazards |———————————| Safe environment

NOTE IF ANYBODY DISAGREES WITH THIS ASSESSMENT

146

Education

5–9 years

The questions in this section are designed to make sure that the child's educational attainments are average or above and that s/he acquires special skills and interests and takes a full part in school activities

E 1 How well is the child doing at school?

Reading:

☐ Poor ☐ Below average ☐ Average
☐ Above average ☐ Excellent ☐ Don't know

Writing:

☐ Poor ☐ Below average ☐ Average
☐ Above average ☐ Excellent ☐ Don't know

Mathematics:

☐ Poor ☐ Below average ☐ Average
☐ Above average ☐ Excellent ☐ Don't know

If the child is not doing well, i.e. poor performance in all or some of these areas, what further action will be taken?

Who will take it?

☐ Parent ☐ Social Worker ☐ Foster Carer
☐ Residential Worker ☐ Other ☐ No action needed

Explanation for lack of information or no action

E 2 How often does the child go to a library or bring a book home from school?

☐ Once a week ☐ Once a month ☐ Less than once a month

☐ Don't know

If less than once a week, what further action will be taken?

Who will take it?

☐ Parent ☐ Social Worker ☐ Foster Carer
☐ Residential Worker ☐ Other ☐ No action needed

Explanation for lack of information or no action

E 3 Who provides help with school work?

☐ Parent ☐ Social Worker ☐ Foster Carer

☐ Residential Worker ☐ Other ☐ No-one

☐ Don't know

If no-one or don't know, who will take responsibility for helping in the future?

☐ Parent ☐ Social Worker ☐ Foster Carer

☐ Residential Worker ☐ Other ☐ No action needed

Explanation for lack of information or no action

E 4 Whose responsibility is it to discuss the child's school progress with teachers and record decisions taken?

☐ Parent ☐ Social Worker ☐ Foster Carer

☐ Residential Worker ☐ Other ☐ No-one

☐ Don't know

If no-one or don't know, who will take responsibility in the future?

☐ Parent ☐ Social Worker ☐ Foster Carer

☐ Residential Worker ☐ Other ☐ No action needed

Explanation for lack of information or no action

E 5 Who attends school events and parents' evenings?

☐ Parent ☐ Social Worker ☐ Foster Carer

☐ Residential Worker ☐ Other ☐ No-one

☐ Don't know

If no-one attends, who will go in the future?

☐ Parent ☐ Social Worker ☐ Foster Carer

☐ Residential Worker ☐ Other ☐ No action needed

Explanation for lack of information or no action

E 6 Does the child go to school regularly?

☐ Yes ☐ No ☐ Don't know

If no or don't know, what further action will be taken?

Who will take it?

☐ Parent ☐ Social Worker ☐ Foster Carer

☐ Residential Worker ☐ Other ☐ No action needed

Explanation for lack of information or no action

148

E 7 What non-classroom activities has the
child participated in?
(e.g. outings/clubs/sports)

If none, what further action will be taken?

Who will take it?

☐ Parent   ☐ Social Worker   ☐ Foster Carer

☐ Residential Worker ☐ Other   ☐ No action needed

Explanation for lack of information or no action

E 8 Which of the following has the child
learnt to do?

Swim   ☐ Yes   ☐ No   ☐ Don't know

Ride a bicycle   ☐ Yes   ☐ No   ☐ Don't know

Begin to play a musical instrument ☐ Yes   ☐ No   ☐ Don't know

Does the child have other skills or
hobbies, not detailed above? Specify:

What further action is needed to encourage these?

Who will take it?

☐ Parent   ☐ Social Worker   ☐ Foster Carer

☐ Residential Worker ☐ Other   ☐ No action needed

Explanation for lack of information or no action

E 9 Have learning disabilities been noted?

☐ Yes ☐ No ☐ Don't know

If so, have these been recorded?

☐ Yes ☐ No ☐ Don't know

☐ Not applicable

If disabilities have been recognised, what extra help is the child receiving?

What further action is needed?

Who will take it?

☐ Parent ☐ Social Worker ☐ Foster Carer

☐ Residential Worker ☐ Other ☐ No action needed

Explanation for lack of information or no action

E 10 How many unscheduled changes of school has the child experienced since the involvement of the social services department? (*see guidelines*)

☐ Number ☐ Don't know

Have all changes of school been recorded?

☐ Yes ☐ No ☐ Don't know

What action has been taken to encourage continuity?

Who will take further action if necessary?

☐ Parent ☐ Social Worker ☐ Foster Carer

☐ Residential Worker ☐ Other ☐ No action needed

Explanation for lack of information or no action

150

HAVE THE FOLLOWING AIMS
BEEN ACHIEVED?

AE1 The child's educational
attainments are average or above

All well below | | All well above
average | | average

AE 2 The child is acquiring special
skills and interests

None | | Many

AE 3 The child is participating fully in
school activities

Not at all | | Fully

AE 4 The child is favourably regarded
by teachers

Very | | Very favourably
unfavourably

NOTE IF ANYBODY DISAGREES
WITH THIS ASSESSMENT

I Identity   5–9 years

The questions in this section are designed to make sure that the child has
the opportunity to develop self-esteem, an understanding of his/her current
situation, and some knowledge of the characteristics of his/her birth family
and ethnic background.

I 1 Can the child give his/her full name,
address and birthday?

☐ Yes   ☐ No   ☐ Don't know

If no, or don't know, who will take
further action?

☐ Parent   ☐ Social Worker   ☐ Foster Carer

☐ Residential Worker ☐ Other ☐ No action needed

Explanation for lack of information or no action

I 2 Can the child explain why s/he is not living with own parents?

☐ Yes   ☐ No   ☐ Don't know

☐ Not applicable

If no, or don't know, who will take further action?

☐ Parent   ☐ Social Worker   ☐ Foster Carer

☐ Residential Worker   ☐ Other   ☐ No action needed

Explanation for lack of information or no action

I 3 Has an up-to-date life story book been made, and discussed with the child?

☐ Yes   ☐ No   ☐ Don't know

If no, or don't know, who will take further action?

☐ Parent   ☐ Social Worker   ☐ Foster Carer

☐ Residential Worker   ☐ Other   ☐ No action needed

Explanation for lack of information or no action

I 4 How many members of his/her family of origin or adoptive family can the child name?

☐ Number   ☐ Don't know

What further action is needed?

Who will take it?

☐ Parent   ☐ Social Worker   ☐ Foster Carer

☐ Residential Worker   ☐ Other   ☐ No action needed

Explanation for lack of information or no action

I 5 Does the child have contact with other adults/children who come from the same ethnic background?

☐ Daily   ☐ Several times a month   ☐ Less than once a month

☐ Don't know

Question **I 5** continues overleaf

152

Question **I 5** continues

If less than once a month, or don't know, what further action will be taken?

Who will take it?

☐ Parent   ☐ Social Worker   ☐ Foster Carer
☐ Residential Worker ☐ Other   ☐ No action needed

Explanation for lack of information or no action

I 6 Is the child aware of the customs and religion of his/her family of origin?

☐ Yes   ☐ No   ☐ Don't know

What further action will be taken?

Who will take it?

☐ Parent   ☐ Social Worker   ☐ Foster Carer
☐ Residential Worker ☐ Other   ☐ No action needed

Explanation for lack of information or no action

I 7 What has the carer done to protect the child against discrimination?

What further action will be taken?

Who will take it?

☐ Parent   ☐ Social Worker   ☐ Foster Carer
☐ Residential Worker ☐ Other   ☐ No action needed

Explanation for lack of information or no action

I 8 What is the child's attitude to his/her racial/ethnic identity?

☐ Positive   ☐ Mixed   ☐ Negative
☐ Unaware of ethnic identity   ☐ Don't know

What further action is needed?

Question **I 8** continues overleaf

153

Question **I 8** continues

Who will take it?

☐ Parent   ☐ Social Worker   ☐ Foster Carer

☐ Residential Worker   ☐ Other   ☐ No action needed

Explanation for lack of information or no action

I 9 If the child is separated from his/her birth family, are foster carers and birth parents open about their relationship to him or her?

☐ Yes   ☐ Some concealment   ☐ No

☐ Don't know   ☐ Not applicable

Who will take further action if necessary?

☐ Parent   ☐ Social Worker   ☐ Foster Carer

☐ Residential Worker   ☐ Other   ☐ No action needed

Explanation for lack of information or no action

I 10 Does the child receive loving approval?

☐ Often   ☐ Sometimes   ☐ Seldom

☐ Don't know

If the child receives little or no praise, why is this?

Who will take further action?

☐ Parent   ☐ Social Worker   ☐ Foster Carer

☐ Residential Worker   ☐ Other   ☐ No action needed

Explanation for lack of information or no action

I 11 What does the child consider her/himself to be good at?

If nothing, what further action will be taken?

Who will take it?

☐ Parent   ☐ Social Worker   ☐ Foster Carer

☐ Residential Worker   ☐ Other   ☐ No action needed

Explanation for lack of information or no action

HAVE THE FOLLOWING AIMS
BEEN ACHIEVED?

AI 1 The child has positive self-
esteem

Low self-esteem |————————| High self-esteem

AI 2 The child has an understanding
of his/her current care situation

Unaware |————————| Clear understanding

AI 3 The child has knowledge of his/
her family of origin

No knowledge |————————| Thorough knowledge

AI 4 The child can recognise and
relate to his/her ethnic
background

Not at all |————————| Very easily

NOTE IF ANYBODY DISAGREES
WITH THIS ASSESSMENT

F ## Family and Social Relationships 5–9 years

The questions in this section are designed to check that, as far as possible,
the child has long-term continuity of care, that s/he has the opportunity to
develop close emotional ties with at least one caregiver, that s/he regularly
sees those members of his or her family of origin who have access, and
that s/he is accepted by adults and other children.

F1 How many placements involving a
change of caregiver has the child
experienced since his or her last
admission to local authority care/
accommodation? (Include current
placement, and also periods spent at
home with relatives or friends; do not
include short holidays of less than **two
weeks** or hospital admissions)

[ ] Number   [ ] Don't know

Explanation for lack of information

155

F 2 How does the child get on with his/ her current carers?

☐ Poorly ☐ No obvious problems ☐ Very well

Does anybody disagree with this assessment? (If anybody thinks the relationship is poor, please describe)

What further action is needed?

Who will take it?

☐ Parent ☐ Social Worker ☐ Foster Carer
☐ Residential Worker ☐ Other ☐ No action needed

Explanation for lack of information or no action

F 3 Does the principal carer show physical affection to the child?

☐ Often ☐ Sometimes ☐ Seldom
☐ Don't know

If seldom or don't know, what further action will be taken?

Who will take it?

☐ Parent ☐ Social Worker ☐ Foster Carer
☐ Residential Worker ☐ Other ☐ No action needed

Explanation for lack of information or no action

F 4 Has the child had continuing contact with at least one adult throughout his/ her life?

☐ Yes ☐ No ☐ Don't know

Has this person's name and address been recorded?

☐ Yes ☐ No ☐ Don't know
☐ Not applicable

Who will take further action if needed?

☐ Parent ☐ Social Worker ☐ Foster Carer
☐ Residential Worker ☐ Other ☐ No action needed

Explanation for lack of information or no action

F5 How frequently does the child see the following?:

	At least weekly	Less than weekly but at least monthly	Less than monthly/ irregularly	Never	Don't know
Mother	☐	☐	☐	☐	☐
Father	☐	☐	☐	☐	☐
Other persons with parental responsibility	☐	☐	☐	☐	☐
Grandparents if not included above	☐	☐	☐	☐	☐
Brothers and sisters	☐	☐	☐	☐	☐
Previous carers	☐	☐	☐	☐	☐
Others (specify):	☐	☐	☐	☐	☐

Is further action needed to promote these relationships? ☐ Yes ☐ No ☐ Don't know

Who will take it?

☐ Parent   ☐ Social Worker   ☐ Foster Carer

☐ Residential Worker   ☐ Other   ☐ No action needed

Explanation for lack of information or no action

Describe any contacts which do not appear beneficial to the child:

What further action will be taken?

Who will take it?

☐ Parent   ☐ Social Worker   ☐ Foster Carer

☐ Residential Worker   ☐ Other   ☐ No action needed

Explanation for lack of information or no action

If the child has insufficient contact with a birth parent have steps been taken to develop a close relationship with another adult relative or friend?   ☐ Yes ☐ No ☐ Don't know

☐ Not applicable

What further action will be taken?

Question **F 5** continues overleaf

157

Question **F 5** continues

Who will take it?

☐ Parent	☐ Social Worker	☐ Foster Carer
☐ Residential Worker	☐ Other	☐ No action needed

Explanation for lack of information or no action

F 6 Are contact arrangements being complied with by all those concerned?

☐ Yes   ☐ No   ☐ Don't know

☐ Not applicable

If not, please describe.

What further action will be taken?

Who will take it?

☐ Parent	☐ Social Worker	☐ Foster Carer
☐ Residential Worker	☐ Other	☐ No action needed

Explanation for lack of information or no action

F 7 Can the child tell you who are his/her special friends?

☐ Yes   ☐ No   ☐ Don't know

If s/he says s/he has none, what further action will be taken?

Who will take it?

☐ Parent	☐ Social Worker	☐ Foster Carer
☐ Residential Worker	☐ Other	☐ No action needed

Explanation for lack of information or no action

F 8 What opportunities does the child have for out-of-school contact with friends?

☐ Frequent   ☐ Rare   ☐ Very rare

☐ No friends   ☐ Don't know

What further action will be taken?

Who will take it?

☐ Parent	☐ Social Worker	☐ Foster Carer
☐ Residential Worker	☐ Other	☐ No action needed

Explanation for lack of information or no action

158

HAVE THE FOLLOWING AIMS
BEEN ACHIEVED?

AF 1 The child has had long-term
continuity of care

Care seriously _____ Continuous
disrupted   care since last
                                       admission

AF 2 The child has close emotional
ties with at least one caregiver

No clear _____ Strong
attachment   attachment

AF 3 The child has regular contacts
with those members of family of
origin who have access

Few or no _____ All contacts
contacts   well
                                 maintained

☐ Not applicable

AF 4 The child is accepted by adults
and other children

Unpopular _____ Popular

AF 5 The child is beginning to form
stable friendships   ☐ Yes   ☐ Doubtful   ☐ No

☐ Don't know

NOTE IF ANYBODY DISAGREES
WITH THIS ASSESSMENT

P **Social Presentation**   5–9 years

The questions in this section are designed to make sure that the child's
appearance and behaviour make a good impression on others and that
s/he is learning to adjust them to different contexts.

P 1 Does the child appear well cared for?
     ☐ Yes   ☐ Not very   ☐ No
     ☐ Don't know

If not, please describe

Question **P** 1 continues overleaf

159

Question **P 1** continues

Who will take further action if necessary?

☐ Parent ☐ Social Worker ☐ Foster Carer

☐ Residential Worker ☐ Other ☐ No action needed

Explanation for lack of information or no action

P 2 Are the child's clothes appropriate to his/her age and peer-group?

☐ Yes ☐ Not very ☐ No

☐ Don't know

If not, please describe

Who will take further action if necessary?

☐ Parent ☐ Social Worker ☐ Foster Carer

☐ Residential Worker ☐ Other ☐ No action needed

Explanation for lack of information or no action

P 3 Can other children and adults understand what the child says?

☐ Always ☐ Usually ☐ Sometimes

☐ Rarely ☐ Don't know

If not always, what further action is needed?

Who will take it?

☐ Parent ☐ Social Worker ☐ Foster Carer

☐ Residential Worker ☐ Other ☐ No action needed

Explanation for lack of information or no action

P 4 Has the child learnt to say please, thank you, excuse me, etc.?

☐ Yes ☐ Doubtful ☐ No

☐ Don't know

Who will take further action if necessary?

☐ Parent ☐ Social Worker ☐ Foster Carer

☐ Residential Worker ☐ Other ☐ No action needed

Explanation for lack of information or no action

160

P 5 Can the child adjust behaviour/
conversation to an increasingly wide
range of situations: e.g. other homes,
public transport, places of
entertainment?

☐ Yes   ☐ Not always   ☐ No

☐ Don't know

If unsatisfactory, please describe

Who will take further action if
necessary?

☐ Parent   ☐ Social Worker   ☐ Foster Carer

☐ Residential Worker   ☐ Other   ☐ No action needed

Explanation for lack of information or no action

**HAVE THE FOLLOWING AIMS
BEEN ACHIEVED?**

AP 1 The child's appearance and
behaviour are acceptable to
peers and adults

Not at all |—————————————| Very acceptable

AP 2 The child can communicate
easily with others

With great
difficulty |—————————————| Very easily

AP 3 The child is learning to adjust
appearance and manners to
different contexts

Not at all |—————————————| Good
adjustment

**NOTE IF ANYBODY DISAGREES
WITH THIS ASSESSMENT**

The questions in this section are designed to make sure that action is being
taken to monitor and correct emotional and behavioural problems

B 1 Does the child display any of the
following?

(a) Eating problems Often ├────────────────┤ Never ☐ Don't know

(b) Sleeping problems Often ├────────────────┤ Never ☐ Don't know

(c) Marked clinging Often ├────────────────┤ Never ☐ Don't know

(d) Fearfulness Often ├────────────────┤ Never ☐ Don't know

(e) Extremely quiet Often ├────────────────┤ Never ☐ Don't know

(f) Excessive shyness Often ├────────────────┤ Never ☐ Don't know

(g) Wet by day or night Often ├────────────────┤ Never ☐ Don't know

(h) Soiling Often ├────────────────┤ Never ☐ Don't know

(i) Irritability Often ├────────────────┤ Never ☐ Don't know

(j) Tantrums Often ├────────────────┤ Never ☐ Don't know

(k) Aggressiveness Often ├────────────────┤ Never ☐ Don't know

(l) Disinclination to play Often ├────────────────┤ Never ☐ Don't know

Question **P 1** continues overleaf

Question **B 1** continues

(m) Truancy

Often |————————————| Never ☐ Don't know

(n) Stealing

Often |————————————| Never ☐ Don't know

(o) Lying/fantasy

Often |————————————| Never ☐ Don't know

(p) Inappropriate sexual behaviour

Often |————————————| Never ☐ Don't know

(q) Other problems

Specify:

Often |————————————| Never ☐ Don't know

Please describe problem(s):

How is it/are they being dealt with at present?

What further action is needed?

Who will take it?

☐ Parent   ☐ Social Worker   ☐ Foster Carer

☐ Residential Worker   ☐ Other   ☐ No action needed

Explanation for lack of information or no action

B 2 Is the child able to get on with unknown adults without being over-friendly or attention-seeking?

☐ Yes   ☐ No   ☐ Don't know

What further action is needed?

Question **B 3** continues overleaf

Question **B 2** continues

Who will take it?

☐ Parent ☐ Social Worker ☐ Foster Carer

☐ Residential Worker ☐ Other ☐ No action needed

Explanation for lack of information or no action

B 3 Has the child experienced abuse?
(e.g. physical abuse, sexual abuse,
severe bullying)

☐ Definitely ☐ Suspected ☐ No suspicions

☐ Don't know

If so, what further protection and/or help does s/he need?

Who will take further action if
necessary?

☐ Parent ☐ Social Worker ☐ Foster Carer

☐ Residential Worker ☐ Other ☐ No action needed

Explanation for lack of information or no action

**HAVE THE FOLLOWING AIMS
BEEN ACHIEVED?**

AB 1 **The child is free of serious
emotional and behavioural
problems**

Serious
problems exist |————————————————| No problems

AB2 **The child is receiving effective
treatment for all persistent
problems**

Not receiving
enough help |————————————————| Receiving
effective
treatment

☐ Not applicable

**NOTE IF ANYBODY DISAGREES
WITH THIS ASSESSMENT**

| **S** | **Self-Care Skills** | 5–9 years |

The questions in this section are designed to make sure that the child is learning to care for him/herself with some supervision.

(If you have filled in this form for this child before, you need only check the skills s/he had not yet mastered at the time of the previous assessment; the child would only be expected to have mastered all these skills by the time s/he reaches the top of the age-range)

S 1 Which of the following can the child do?

	Fully mastered	Learning	Not learning	Don't know
(a) Clean teeth without being told	☐	☐	☐	☐
(b) Bath self	☐	☐	☐	☐
(c) Make bed	☐	☐	☐	☐
(d) Get a drink or snack for him/herself	☐	☐	☐	☐
(e) Wash up	☐	☐	☐	☐
(f) Be aware of common hazards such as poisons, tools, electricity, fires	☐	☐	☐	☐
(g) Answer the telephone	☐	☐	☐	☐
(h) Make an emergency telephone call	☐	☐	☐	☐
(i) Handle small amounts of money	☐	☐	☐	☐
(j) Cross quiet roads safely	☐	☐	☐	☐

In the case of skills not being taught or lack of information

Who will take further action?

☐ Parent ☐ Social Worker ☐ Foster Carer

☐ Residential Worker ☐ Other ☐ No action needed

Explanation for lack of information or no action

HAS THE FOLLOWING AIM BEEN ACHIEVED?

AS1 The child is learning to care for him/herself with some supervision

| **Child not yet competent to care for self with supervision** | | **Child competent to care for self with some supervision** |

NOTE IF ANYBODY DISAGREES WITH THIS ASSESSMENT

SUMMARY OF WORK TO BE UNDERTAKEN

	Work required	Person responsible	Target date	Date completed
HEALTH				
EDUCATION				
IDENTITY				
FAMILY AND SOCIAL RELATIONSHIPS				
SOCIAL PRESENTATION				
EMOTIONAL AND BEHAVIOURAL DEVELOPMENT				
SELF-CARE SKILLS				

Printed in the United Kingdom for HMSO Dd. 295207 C15 10/91

166

Appendix Three

Basic Facts Sheet for Child or Young Person Looked After by Local Authority

---

I PERSONAL DETAILS

1 Date sheet first completed

2 Dates of updating

3 File reference number

4 Child's name (underline names normally used and include any others by which child may be known)

Surname

Forenames

5 Address

Postcode

Telephone

6 Sex

7 Date of birth

7(a) Where is the birth certificate kept?

Tick box if certificate has been seen by social worker

8 Place of birth

9 Ethnic origin

10 Religion

practising / nominal (delete as appropriate)

11 First language

11(a) Does child speak and understand English?   yes   no

12 Court orders currently affecting the child (note both civil and criminal, and include orders made in respect of parents)

(a) Before local authority supervision

Date	Court	Type of order	Reason	Duration	Where is the order kept?

12(b) Since local authority supervision

Date	Court	Type of order	Reason	Duration	Where is the order kept?

II FAMILY DETAILS

13 Mother's name (underline names normally used and include any others by which mother may be known)

Surname

Forenames

Date of birth and / or age

Address (if different from child)

Postcode

Telephone

14 Father's name (underline names normally used and include any others by which father may be known)

Surname

Forename

Date of birth and / or age

Address (if different from child)

Postcode

Telephone

14(a) Does the father have parental responsibility?

yes ☐   no ☐

15 Brothers and sisters

Name	Date of birth or age	Address

16 Other significant adults (eg grandparents, step-parents)   Does this person have parental responsibility?

Name	Relationship	Address	Yes / No

NB If any of the above have parental responsibility check that the full details have been recorded at section 12 above

III HEALTH

17 GP's name

Address

Postcode

Telephone

18 Health Visitor's name

Address

Postcode

Telephone

19 Dentist's name

Address

Postcode

Telephone

20 Community Paediatrician's name

Address

Postcode

Telephone

21 Other professional contacts

Name

Occupation

Address

Postcode

Telephone

22 NHS number

22(a) Where is the card kept?

169

23 Immunisations

Age due	Immunisations * delete if pertussis omitted	Age given
2 months	Diphtheria/Tetanus/Pertussis (Whooping cough)* /Polio	
3 months	Diphtheria/Tetanus/Pertussis (Whooping cough)* /Polio	
4 months	Diphtheria/Tetanus/Pertussis (Whooping cough)* /Polio	
12 - 18 months	Measles/Mumps/Rubella	
4 - 5 years	Diphtheria/Tetanus/Polio	
4 - 5 years	Measles/Mumps/Rubella (if not yet given)	
10 - 14 years	Rubella (girls only; not necessary if MMR has been given)	
10 - 14 years	Heaf test and BCG	
15 - 18 years	Tetanus/Polio	

Other immunisations (please specify)

23(a) Have any immunisations been omitted because of medical contra-indications? yes ☐ no ☐

If yes, which?

24 Allergies

25 Childhood illnesses (tick if child has had any of the following)

Age contracted if known

(a) Measles ☐

(b) German measles (Rubella) ☐

(c) Chicken pox ☐

(d) Whooping cough (Pertussis) ☐

(e) Mumps ☐

Other significant illnesses — Age contracted if known

26 Chronic conditions/disabilities (tick if child suffers from any of the following; add • if severe)

Condition/disability	Tick	•	Age at diagnosis years months
Diabetes	☐	☐	
Asthma	☐	☐	
Eczema	☐	☐	
Glue ear	☐	☐	
Coeliac disease	☐	☐	
Cystic fibrosis	☐	☐	
Juvenile rheumatoid arthritis	☐	☐	
Sickle cell disease	☐	☐	
Thalassaemia	☐	☐	
Visual impairment	☐	☐	
Hearing impairment	☐	☐	
Learning difficulties	☐	☐	

Other (please specify)

170

27 Periods in hospital

Dates from	to	Hospital	Reason	Consultant

IV EDUCATION

28 Name of current Head Teacher

Telephone

29 Name of current Class Teacher

Telephone

30 Education Social Worker

Telephone

31 Educational Psychologist

Telephone

	yes	no	pending

32 Has the child been made the subject of a statement of special educational needs under the Education Act 1981 ? ☐ ☐ ☐

33 Schools attended (from age five)

Dates from	to	Name	Type	Reason for leaving

171

34 Educational qualifications:

GCSE (or equivalent)

Subject	Grade

A level (or equivalent)

Subject	Grade

35 Other academic or vocational qualifications

36 Other achievements (sport, music, drama etc.)

37 Other courses and training undertaken

37(a) If the young person has left school with no academic qualifications, or none known, tick box

No academic qualifications ☐

No academic qualifications known ☐

38 Full-time employment since leaving school

Tick if government training scheme

Dates from	to	Occupation	

172

VI RECORD OF PLACEMENTS WHILE BEING LOOKED AFTER OR SUPERVISED BY LOCAL AUTHORITY: (include periods spent at home with relatives or friends; do not include short holidays of less than a week, or hospital admissions)

Name of foster carer / residential establishment	Address	Dates from	to	Reason for leaving

Developed by the School of Applied Social Studies, University of Bristol in conjunction with the Department of Health.

© Crown copyright 1991   First published 1991   Second impression (with amendments) 1992

Applications for reproduction should be made to HMSO

Plan for Child or Young Person
Looked After by Local Authority

(To be completed as part of the admission procedure, and to be fully discussed at first
statutory review (i.e. four weeks after child enters local authority care/accommodation)

I   BASIC INFORMATION

1   Child's surname

Child's forename(s)

2   File reference number

3   Date of birth

4   Sex

5   Present legal status of child

6   Address from which admitted

Postcode

Name of previous carer

Relationship to child

7   Date of admission

8   Date this form completed

9   Name of social worker

10   Social worker's workbase

Telephone

11   Who shares the parental responsibility for this child?

12   Are the names and addresses of
mother, father and other significant
adults adequately recorded on the
file?

Yes   No   Don't Know

If no, please explain:

175

II BACKGROUND TO CURRENT SITUATION

13 Support already offered to the family — Please tick where appropriate

(a) Informal social work supervision/support ☐

(b) Statutory supervision order for this child ☐

(c) Statutory supervision order for another child/other children in the family ☐

(d) Financial assistance ☐

(e) Nursery care ☐

(f) Respite care for this child ☐

(g) Respite care for another child/other children in the family ☐

(h) Care/accommodation for this child ☐

(i) Care/accommodation for another child/other chidren in the family ☐

(j) Family centre/day care ☐

Other
(Specify) _____

14 Reason(s) for current involvement

_____
_____
_____
_____
_____
_____
_____
_____

15 What other agencies have been consulted concerning this child's current situation and the formulation of this plan?
Please give details of any relevant information from other agencies. Any written reports should be attached to this plan

_____
_____
_____
_____
_____
_____
_____
_____
_____
_____

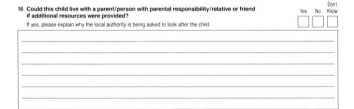

**16 Could this child live with a parent/person with parental responsibility/relative or friend
if additional resources were provided?**

Yes ☐ No ☐ Don't Know ☐

If yes, please explain why the local authority is being asked to look after the child

_____
_____
_____
_____
_____
_____

176

III THE PLAN

17 Intermediate objectives of this intervention
Please specify:

(a) What arrangements will be made to meet the child's health requirements?

Who will have the authority to give consent to the child's medical treatment?

Has this issue been discussed with the parents, the carers and the child if of sufficient age and understanding?   Yes ☐   No ☐

(b) What arrangements will be made to meet the child's educational requirements?

(c) What arrangements will be made to meet needs arising from the child's race, religion, culture or language?

(d) Any other arrangements which need to be made?

(e) What part of the child's everyday care will be undertaken by the parents?

18 Long-term objectives for the child
Please tick where appropriate

(a) Restoration to birth/family ☐

(b) Restoration to other relatives ☐

(c) Permanent substitute care:
  (i) Long-term foster care ☐
  (ii) Adoption with contact ☐
  (iii) Adoption without contact ☐

(d) Supported living in the community ☐

(e) Independent living ☐

Other
(Specify)

19 Plan of work required to achieve these objectives

(a) With child

Proposed timescale

Person(s) responsible

(b) With parents/relatives

Proposed timescale

Person(s) responsible

177

19 continued

(c) With others (specify)

Proposed timescale

Person(s) responsible

20 Legal action required (if any)

21 What placement is proposed/has been arranged?

Placement type

Name(s) of carers

Relationship (if any) to child

Address

Postcode

Telephone

22 Does this placement

	Yes	No

(a) *meet the child's needs?
(including the particular needs described
in section 17 above)

(b) *meet the requirements of the plan?

*If no, please indicate what alterations are necessary
(e.g. additional assistance from the local authority, change
of placement, special services)

**23 Details of any special financial implications of these
arrangements**

**24 For how long will the child need to be looked after
away from home?**

**25 What is the contingency plan if the preferred
placement/additional assistance is not obtainable?**

IV CONTACT

26 Is/Are any person(s) to be refused contact?
Yes　No　Don't Know
☐　☐　☐

If yes, specify names and addresses here

Name _____
Address _____
Postcode _____

Is it necessary to apply for an order under the Children Act 1989, Section 34?

Yes　No
☐　☐

Name _____
Address _____
Postcode _____

Name _____
Address _____
Postcode _____

27 Contact arrangements for others

Person in contact	Type (visit/letter etc)	Place of visits	Frequency of visits	Section 8 order?
Mother				
Father				
Brother(s)/Sister(s)				
Person(s) with parental responsibility				
Others (specify)				

28 Have all persons who have contact been given the child's address?
Yes　No　Don't Know
☐　☐　☐

If no, please explain
_____

29 Has the child (if of sufficient age and understanding) been given the addresses of all persons who have contact?
Yes　No　Don't Know
☐　☐　☐

If no, please explain
_____

30 Have the carers been given the addresses of all persons who have contact?
Yes　No　Don't Know
☐　☐　☐

If no, please explain
_____

V CONSULTATION

31 **Have the plan and contact arrangements been discussed with:** (Please tick where appropriate)

(a) The child? ☐   (b) The child's mother? ☐   (c) The child's father? ☐

(d) Other person(s) with parental responsibility? ☐   (e) Other interested friends and relatives named above? ☐   (f) Foster carers/Residential workers? ☐

If the child or parents have difficulty in communicating, what extra resources (eg interpreter/braille/tapes) were provided?

If the proposals have not been discussed with any of the parties concerned, please give reasons

32 **Do all interested parties agree to these proposals?**

Yes ☐   No ☐   Don't Know ☐

Please give details of disagreements; how will they be dealt with?

33 **What steps will be taken if any party decides to alter this arrangement?**

34 **Date and place at which this plan is to be reviewed**

Signatures

Child (if of sufficient age and understanding)	
Mother	
Father	
Other person(s) with parental responsibility	
Other interested relative (if applicable)	
Foster carer/ Residental worker	
Social worker	
Team leader/ Reviewing officer	

Continued overleaf

180

VI ADMINISTRATION

35 **Have copies of this plan been sent to all those invited to sign above?** (Tick box when done)

☐

36 **Have summaries of the plan or notification of arrangements been sent to:** (Tick box when done)

(a) All representatives of other agencies who were consulted concerning these arrangements?

☐

If the child is to be looked after away from home:
(b) All persons specified under Arrangements for Placement of Children (General) Regulations 1991, No. 5?

☐

If the child is in care and about to be placed with parents:
(c) All persons specified under The Placement of Children with Parents etc. Regulations 1991, No. 8?

☐

Developed by the School of Applied Social Studies, University of Bristol in conjunction with the Department of Health

© Crown Copyright 1991
Applications for reproduction should be made to HMSO.
First published 1991
Second impression (with amendments) 1992

HMSO publications are available from:

HMSO Publications Centre
(Mail, fax and telephone orders only)
PO Box 276, London, SW8 5DT
Telephone orders 071-873 9090
General enquiries 071-873 0011
(queuing system in operation for both numbers)
Fax orders 071-873 8200

HMSO Bookshops
49 High Holborn, London, WC1V 6HB
(counter service only)
071-873 0011 Fax 071-873 8200
258 Broad Street, Birmingham, B1 2HE
021-643 3740 Fax 021-643 6510
Southey House, 33 Wine Street, Bristol, BS1 2BQ
0272 264306 Fax 0272 294515
9-21 Princess Street, Manchester, M60 8AS
061-834 7201 Fax 061-833 0634
16 Arthur Street, Belfast, BT1 4GD
0232 238451 Fax 0232 235401
71 Lothian Road, Edinburgh, EH3 9AZ
031-228 4181 Fax 031-229 2734

HMSO's Accredited Agents
(see Yellow Pages)

and through good booksellers

Review of Arrangements for Child or Young Person Looked After by Local Authority

(To be completed at each statutory review of child)

I BASIC INFORMATION

1 Child's surname

Child's forename(s)

2 File reference number

3 Date of birth

4 Sex

5 Present legal status of child

6 Date of initial plan

7 Date of last review

8 Date this form completed

9 Current placement
Placement type

Name of carers

Relationship (if any) to child

Address

Postcode

Telephone

10 Date of last medical examination

If this is outside the statutorily required interval, please explain

11 Dates of social worker's visits to the placement since admission/last review (Underline if child seen)

If these do not meet the statutory requirements, please explain

183

12 Dates of social worker's contacts with the child's relatives since admission/last review
(Underline if mother and father seen together)

Mother	Father	Adult with parental responsibility: (specify)	Other: (specify)

13 Are all names and addresses of the above correctly recorded on file? Yes No Don't Know

If not, please explain

II CHANGES

14 **What changes have there been in the child's circumstances since the initial plan or last review?**

(a) Changes of placement

(b) Significant changes in the child's health (eg diagnosis of chronic illness or altered developmental status)

(c) Changes of school

(d) Changes to the child's legal status

(e) Changes within the child's birth family

(f) Changes within the child's foster family/residential placement

(g) Changes in the child's relationship with parents, relatives, foster carers or residential workers

15 **If the child is in a foster placement, do all members of the foster family welcome the child's presence?**

If no, please specify

Yes   No   Not applicable
☐   ☐   ☐

16 **Would you describe the current placement as** (Tick appropriate box)

Very stable ☐   Stable ☐   Fragile ☐   Approaching breakdown ☐

185

III ACTION

17 When was the basic facts sheet
last updated?

18 When was the assessment and action record
last completed?

19 **Summary of work to be undertaken in the following areas**
(Copy of summary from assessment and action record may be attached here)

(a) Health

Work required	Person responsible	Target date	Completion date

(b) Education

Work required	Person responsible	Target date	Completion date

(c) Identity

Work required	Person responsible	Target date	Completion date

(d) Family and social relationships

Work required	Person responsible	Target date	Completion date

(e) Social presentation

Work required	Person responsible	Target date	Completion date

186

(f) Emotional and behavioural development

Work required	Person responsible	Target date	Completion date

(g) Self-care skills

Work required	Person responsible	Target date	Completion date

20 **Is the current placement within half an hour's journey by foot or public transport of the child's home and siblings?**

Yes ☐ No ☐ Don't Know ☐

If no or don't know, please explain

21 **How well does the current placement meet the child's needs?** (Including special physical and educational needs)

Not at all ☐   Not very well ☐   Satisfactorily ☐   Very well ☐

If unsatisfactory, please explain

22 **If the current placement appears to be unsatisfactory, what alternative plans have been considered?**

IV REVIEW OF PLAN

23 Are there any additional comments about the plan and/or placement? (These may be submitted in writing, prior to the review)

(a) From the child

(b) From the child's mother

(c) From the child's father

(d) From any other adult with parental responsibility

(e) From the carers

(f) From the independent visitor, if appointed

(g) From any other adults concerned with the child. Specify:

23 Continued

Please explain if any of the above have not been consulted and/or have not been invited to the review

24 Do the objectives of the intervention still remain the same?

Yes No

If no, please state new objectives

25 Do the current arrangements meet the objectives of the intervention?

Yes No

If no, describe what further action will be taken, who will take it, and when

26 What work is still necessary to achieve those objectives?
(State proposed time-scales and persons responsible)

(a) With the child

(b) With his/her parents

(c) With the foster-carers/ adoptive parents/placement agency

(d) With others

189

27 Could the child live with a parent/person with parental responsibility/relative or friend if additional resources were provided?

Yes No Don't Know

If yes, please explain why the local authority is being asked to look after the child

28 Has the child been given information concerning his/her rights under the 1989 Children Act?

29 Should any changes be made to contact arrangements?

Yes No Don't Know

If yes, what?

30 Should an independent visitor be appointed?

31 Should steps be taken to secure the discharge or variation of any current order?

Yes No Don't Know

If yes, what?

Person responsible

32 Should any new order be sought? (eg residence order)

Yes No Don't Know

If yes, please specify

Person responsible

33 For how much longer is it expected that the child will be looked after by the local authority?

34 Will the child continue to need assistance after he/she ceases to be looked after by the local authority?

Yes No Don't Know

If yes, please specify

35 Who was invited to this review?

Name	Position	Tick if present

If the child or parents have difficulty in communicating, what extra resources (e.g. interpreter/braille/tapes) were provided?

36 Do all interested parties agree to any alterations to the current plan?   Yes   No

If no, please specify

37 Reviewing officer's comments

_____
_____
_____
_____
_____
_____
_____
_____
_____
_____
_____
_____
_____
_____
_____
_____
_____
_____
_____
_____
_____
_____
_____
_____
_____
_____
_____

Signature

Chair/Reviewing Officer

Date, Time and Venue of next review

Copies of this form, when completed, to be sent to

Child	☐	Mother	☐	Father	☐
Other adults with parental responsibility	☐	Carers	☐	Other participants at review	☐
Other (specify)					☐
					☐
					☐

Developed by the School of Applied Social Studies, University of Bristol in conjunction with the Department of Health

HMSO publications are available from:

HMSO Publications Centre
(Mail, fax and telephone orders only)
PO Box 276, London, SW8 5DT
Telephone orders 071-873 9090
General enquiries 071-873 0011
(queuing system in operation for both numbers)
Fax orders 071-873 8200

HMSO Bookshops
49 High Holborn, London, WC1V 6HB
(counter service only)
071-873 0011 Fax 071-873 8200
258 Broad Street, Birmingham, B1 2HE
021-643 3740 Fax 021-643 6510
Southey House, 33 Wine Street, Bristol, BS1 2BQ
0272 264306 Fax 0272 294515
9-21 Princess Street, Manchester, M60 8AS
061-834 7201 Fax 061-833 0634
16 Arthur Street, Belfast, BT1 4GD
0232 238451 Fax 0232 235401
71 Lothian Road, Edinburgh, EH3 9AZ
031-228 4181 Fax 031-229 2734

HMSO's Accredited Agents
(see Yellow Pages)

and through good booksellers

Bibliography

Aldgate, J. (1976) 'The child in care and his parents', *Adoption and Fostering*, Vol. 84, No. 2.

Aldgate, J. (1977) 'Identification of factors influencing children's length of stay in care', Ph.D. thesis, University of Edinburgh. Summarised in Triseliotis, J. (ed) (1980) *New Developments in Foster Care and Adoption*, London, Routledge and Kegan Paul.

Aldgate, J., Maluccio, A.N., and Reeves, C. (1989) *Adolescents in Foster Families*, London, Batsford.

Arden, N. (1977) *Child of a System*, London, Quartet Books.

Berndt, T. and Ladd, G. (eds) (1989), *Peer Relationships in Child Development*, New York, Wiley.

Berridge, D. (1985) *Children's Homes*, Oxford, Blackwell.

Berridge, D. and Cleaver, H. (1987) *Foster Home Breakdown*, Oxford, Blackwell.

Blaxter, M. (1981) *The Health of the Children: a Review of Research on the Place of Health in Cycles of Disadvantage*, SSRC/DHSS Studies in Deprivation and Disadvantage, London, Heinemann Educational Books.

Bonnerjea, L. (1990) *Leaving Care in London*, London Boroughs Children's Regional Planning Committee.

Bowlby, J. (1951) *Maternal Care and Mental Health*, Geneva, WHO; London, HMSO.

Bucowski, W. and Hoza, B. 'Popularity and friendship' in Berndt, T. and Ladd, G. (1989) *Peer Relationships in Child Development*, New York, Wiley.

Bullard, E. and Malos, E. with Parker, R. (1991) *Custodianship: Caring for other People's Children*, London, HMSO.

Bullock, R., Hosie, K., Little, M. and Millham, S. (1990) 'Secure accommodation for very difficult adolescents; some recent research findings', *Journal of Adolescence*, Vol. 13, No. 3. pp 205–215.

Bullock, R., Hosie, K., Little, M. and Millham, S. (1991) 'The research background to the law on parent access to children in care', *Journal of Social Welfare and Family Law*, 2, pp 85–93.

Court Report (1976) *Fit for the Future; The Report of the Committee on Child Health Services*, Cmnd 6684, London, HMSO.

Davies, B. and Knapp, M. (1981) *Old People's Homes and the Production of Welfare*, London, Routledge and Kegan Paul.

Demetri, A. (1982) *The Demetri Papers*, Voice for the Child in Care Papers, No. 2, London, VCC.

Department of the Environment (1981) *Single and Homeless*, London, HMSO.

Department of the Environment, District Audit (1981) *The Provision of Child Care: A Study of Eight Local Authorities in England and Wales—Final Report*, London, HMSO.

Department of Health and Social Security (1985) *Social Work Decisions in Child Care: Recent Research Findings and Their Implications*, London, HMSO.

Department of Health and Social Security (Northern Ireland) (1986) *Report of the Committee of Inquiry into Children's Homes and Hostels*, London, HMSO.

Department of Health (1989a) *An Introduction to the Children Act 1989*, London, HMSO.

Department of Health (1989b) *The Diets of British Schoolchildren*, London, HMSO.

Department of Health (1991) *The Children Act 1989: Guidance and Regulations*, London, HMSO.

Dickinson, J. (1988) 'Sour smell that is Stephen's legacy of a life in care', *The Guardian*, 18.8.88.

Dingwall, R., Eekelaar, J. and Murray, T. (1988) *The Protection of Children: State Intervention and Family Life*, Oxford, Blackwell.

Dion, K. and Bercheid, E. (1974) 'Physical attractiveness and peer perception among children', *Sociometry*, Vol. 37, 1–12.

Douglas, J. (1964) *The Home and the School: A Study of Ability and Attainment in the Primary School*, London, Macgibbon and Kee.

Erikson, E. (1963) *Children and Society*, Harmondsworth, Penguin.

Essen, J. and Wedge, P. (1986) *Continuities in Childhood Disadvantage*, Aldershot, Gower.

Farmer, E. and Parker, R.A. (1991) *Trials and Tribulations: Returning Children from Local Authority Care to their Families*, London, HMSO.

Festinger, T. (1983) *No One Ever Asked Us: A Postscript to Foster Care*, New York, Columbia University Press.

Finch, J. (1986) *Research and Policy: the Uses of Qualitative Methods in Social and Educational Research*, London, Falmer Press.

Fisher, M., Marsh, P. and Phillips, D. with Sainsbury, E. (1986) *In and Out of Care: The Experiences of Children, Parents and Social Workers*, London, Batsford, in association with BAAF.

Fletcher-Campbell, F. and Hall, C. (1990) *Changing Schools? Changing People? The Education of Children in Care*, London, National Foundation for Educational Research.

Gardner, R. (1985) *Child Care Reviews*, London, National Children's Bureau.

Gardner, R. (1987) *Who Says? Choice and Control in Care*, London, National Children's Bureau.

George, V. (1970) *Foster Care: Theory and Practice*, London, Routledge and Kegan Paul.

Gibbons, J. (1989) *Purpose and Organisation of Preventive Work with Families: the Two Area Study*, Report for Department of Health.

Hadow Report (1931) *Report of the Consultative Committee on the Primary School*, London, HMSO.

Hardiker, P., Exton, K., and Barker, M. (1989) *Policies and Practices in Preventive Child Care: A Feasibility Study*, University of Leicester School of Social Work.

Hogg, M. and Abrams, D. (1988) *Social Identifications: A Social Psychology of Intergroup Relations and Group Processes*, London, Routledge.

Hoghughi, M. (1978) *Troubled and Troublesome: Coping with Severely Disturbed Children*, London, Burnett Books.

Holman, R. (1980) *Inequality in Child Care*, 2nd Edition, London, Child Poverty Action Group and Family Rights Group.

Hudson, J. and Galaway, B. (eds) (1989) *The State as Parent: International Research Perspectives on Interventions with Young Persons*, Dordrecht, Kluwer Academic Publishers.

Jackson, B. (1964) *Streaming: an Education System in Miniature*, London, Routledge and Kegan Paul.

Jackson, S. (1986) *Education for Children in Care*, in Report of a Scottish Child and Family Alliance Conference held in Dundee, April, 1986.

Jackson, S. (1987) *The Education of Children in Care*, Bristol Papers No. 1, University of Bristol School of Applied Social Studies.

Jackson, S. (1988) *An Evaluation of Education Provision at the NCH Children's Home, Southdowns*, unpublished report for National Children's Home (NCH).

Jackson, S. (1989) 'Residential care and education', *Children and Society* Vol. 4 No. 2, pp 335–350.

Jackson, S. (1991) *Successful in Care*, ongoing research study, funded by the Leverhulme Trust.

Jervis, M. (1990) 'Trans-racial adoption: balancing the damage', *Social Work Today*, 8.2.90.

Kahan, B. (1979) *Growing Up in Care*, Oxford, Blackwell.

Kahan, B. (ed) (1989) *Child Care Research, Policy and Practice*, London, Hodder and Stoughton.

Kenealy, P. et al (1988) 'The influence of children's physical attractiveness on teacher expectations', *Journal of Social Psychology*, Vol. 128 No. 3 pp 373–383.

Knapp, M. (1984) *The Economics of Social Care*, London, Macmillan.

Knapp, M., Bryson, D. and Lewis, J. (1985) *The Objectives of Child Care and their Attainment over a Twelve Month Period for a Cohort of New Admissions*, the Suffolk Cohort Study, Discussion paper 373, PSSRU, University of Kent.

Knapp, M. and Robertson, E. (1989) 'The cost of services', in Kahan, B. (ed) *Child Care Research, Policy and Practice*, London, Hodder and Stoughton.

Lambert, L., Essen, J. and Head, J. (1977) 'Variations in behaviour ratings of children who have been in care', *Journal of Child Psychology and Psychiatry*, 18, pp 335–346.

Lambert, L. (1983) *A Study of the Health of Children in Care using Information Derived from the National Child Development Study*, National Children's Bureau report to the Social Science Research Council.

Lee, J.A.B., 'Promoting competence', in Maluccio (ed) (1981) *Promoting Competence in Clients—a New/Old Approach to Social Work Practice*, New York, The Free Press.

Levy, A. and Kahan, B. (1991) *The Pindown Experience and the Protection of Children: Report of the Staffordshire Child Care Inquiry*, Staffordshire County Council.

Little, M. (1990) *Young Men in Prison: The Criminal Identity Explored through the Rules of Behaviour*, Aldershot, Dartmouth.

MacVeigh, J. (1982) *Gaskin*, London, Cape.

Maluccio, A.N. (ed) (1981) *Promoting Competence in Clients—a New/ Old Approach to Social Work Practice*, New York, the Free Press.

Mayer, J.E. and Timms, N. (1970) *The Client Speaks*, London, Routledge and Kegan Paul.

Mayall, B. (1986) *Keeping Children Healthy: the Role of Mothers and Professionals*, London, Allen and Unwin,

Millham, S., Bullock, R. and Hosie, K. (1978). *Locking up Children*, Aldershot, Saxon House.

Millham, S., Bullock, R., Hosie, K. and Haak, M. (1986). *Lost in Care: the Problem of Maintaining Links Between Children in Care and their Families*, Aldershot, Gower.

Nash, R. (1973) *Classrooms Observed: the Teacher's Perception and the Pupil's Performance*, London, Routledge and Kegan Paul.

National Children's Bureau Children's Policy Review Group (1987) *Investing in the Future; Child Health Ten Years after the Court Report*, London, National Children's Bureau.

Newson, J. and Newson, E. (1977) *Perspectives on School at Seven*, London, Heinemann Educational Books.

Newson, J. and Newson, E. (1968) *Four Years Old in an Urban Community*, London, Allen and Unwin.

Osborn, A. and St. Claire, L. (1987) 'The ability and behaviour of children who have been in care', *Early Child Care and Development*, Vol. 28, No. 3, pp 197–254.

Outcomes Working Party (1988) *Minutes* (Unpublished).

Packman, J., Randall, J. and Jacques, N. (1986) *Who Needs Care? Social Work Decisions about Children*, Oxford, Blackwell.

Page, R. and Clark, G.A. (eds) (1977) *Who Cares? Young People in Care Speak Out*, London, National Children's Bureau.

Parlett, M. and Hamilton, D. (1976) 'Evaluation as illumination: a new approach to the study of innovatory programs', in Glass, G. (ed) *Evaluation Studies Review Annual, Vol. 1*, Beverley Hills, Sage.

Patton, M.Q. (1978) *Utilization-focused Evaluation*, Beverley Hills, Sage.

Parker, R. (1966) *Decision in Child Care*, London, Allen and Unwin.

Parker, R. (1988) 'Residential care for children' in I. Sinclair (ed) *Residential Care, the Research Reviewed*, London, HMSO.

Parker, R. (1990) *Safeguarding Standards*, London, National Institute of Social Work, Joseph Rowntree Memorial Trust.

Parsloe, P. (1981) *Social Services Area Teams*, London, Allen and Unwin.

Pilling, D. (1990) *Escape from Disadvantage*, London, Falmer.

Pinkerton, J. and Kelly, G. (1986) 'Kincora affair—the aftermath', *Youth and Policy*, No. 17.

Quinton, D. and Rutter, M. (1988) *Parenting Breakdown: the Making and Breaking of Intergenerational Links*, Aldershot, Gower.

Reich, D. (1990) Children of the Nightmare', *Adoption and Fostering*, Vol. 14 No. 3.

Rist, R. (1973) *The Urban School: A Factory for Failure*, Cambridge Massachusetts, MIT Press.

Rosser, R. (1983) 'Issues of measurement in the design of health indications: a review' in Culyer, A. J. (ed) *Health Indicators*, Oxford, Martin Robertson.

Rossi, P.H. and Freeman, H.E. (1982) *Evaluation: a Systematic Approach*, Beverley Hills, Sage, (2nd Edition).

Rowe, J., Hundleby, M. and Garnett, L. (1989) *Child Care Now: a Survey of Placement Patterns*, London, BAAF.

Rowe, J. and Lambert, L. (1973) *Children Who Wait*, London, Association of British Adoption Agencies.

Rutter, M. (1967) 'A children's behaviour questionnaire for completion by teachers: preliminary findings', *Journal of Child Psychology and Psychiatry*, Vol. 8, pp 1–11.

Rutter, M. and Giller, H. (1983) *Juvenile Delinquency: Trends and Perspectives*, Harmondsworth, Penguin.

Rutter, M., Quinton, D. and Liddle, C. (1983) 'Parenting in two generations: looking backwards and looking forwards', in Madge N. (ed) *Families at Risk*, London, DHSS.

Rutter, M. (1988) 'Longitudinal data in the study of causal processes: some uses and some pitfalls' in Rutter, M. (ed) *Studies of Psycho-social Risk: the Power of Longitudinal Data*, Cambridge, Cambridge University Press.

Schaffer, H.R. (1984) *The Child's Entry into a Social World*, London, Academic Press.

Sinclair, I. (ed) (1988) *Residential Care: the Research Reviewed*, Vol. 2 of the Wagner Report, London, HMSO.

Sinclair, R. (1984) *Decision-Making in Statutory Reviews on Children in Care*, Aldershot, Gower.

Smith, A. and Jacobson, B. (eds) (1990) *The Nation's Health: a Strategy for the 1990s*, London, King Edward's Hospital Fund for London.

Smith, R. (1987) *Unemployment and Health*, Oxford, Oxford University Press.

Stein, M. and Carey, K. (1986) *Leaving Care*, Oxford, Blackwell.

Stein, M. (1990) *Living Out of Care*, Ilford, Barnardos.

Stevens, S.S. (1946) 'On the theory of scales of measurement', *Science*, Vol. 103, pp 677–680.

Teeling–Smith, G. (ed) (1988) *Measuring Health: a Practical Approach*, Chichester, Wiley.

Thoburn, J. (1990) *Success and Failure in Permanent Family Placement*, Aldershot, Gower.

Tizard, B., Blatchford, P., Burke, J., Farquhar, C. and Plewis, I. (1988) *Young Children at School in the Inner City*, Brighton, Lawrence Erlbaum Associates.

Tizard, B. and Phoenix, A. (1989) 'Black identity and transracial adoption', *New Community*, Vol. 15, (3) pp 427–437. April 1989.

Torrance, G.W. (1986) 'Measurement of health state utilities for economic appraisal', *Journal of Health Economics*, Vol. 5, pp 1–30.

Townsend, P. and Davidson, N. (eds) (1982) *Inequalities in Health: the Black Report*, Harmondsworth, Penguin.

Trasler, G. (1960) *In Place of Parents: a Study of Foster Care*, London, Routledge and Kegan Paul.

Triseliotis, J. (1980a) *Growing up in Foster Care and After*, report submitted to the SSRC.

Triseliotis, J. (ed) (1980b) *New Developments in Foster Care and Adoption*, London, Routledge and Kegan Paul.

Triseliotis, J. and Russell, J. (1984) *Hard to Place: The Outcome of Adoption and Residential Care*, London, Heinemann.

Vernon, J. and Fruin, D. (1986) *In Care: a Study of Social Work Decision-Making*, London, National Children's Bureau.

Ward, H. (1990) *The Charitable Relationship: Parents, Children and the Waifs and Strays Society*, PhD thesis, University of Bristol, (Unpublished).

Ward, H., Jackson, S. and Parker, R. (1991) *A Feasibility Study on the Assessment of Outcomes in Child Care*, Interim report to the Department of Health, University of Bristol.

Ward, H. and Jackson, S. (1991) 'Developing outcome measures in child care: a research note', *British Journal of Social Work*, Vol 21, No 4 pp 393–399.

Webb, S.A. (1990) 'Preventing reception into care: literature review of respite care', *Adoption and Fostering*, Vol. 14, No. 2, pp 21–26.

Wedge, P. and Essen, J. (1982) *Children in Adversity*, London, Heinemann.

Wedge, P. and Phelan, J. (1987) *Essex Child Care Survey, 1981–1985*, Social Work Development Unit, University of East Anglia, Norwich.

Wedge, P. and Mantle, G. (1991) *Sibling Groups and Social Work: a Study of Children Referred for Permanent Substitute Family Placement*, Avebury Academic Publishing Group.

West, D.J. (1967) *The Young Offender*, Harmondsworth, Penguin.

Whitaker, D.S., Cook, J.M., Dunn, C. and Rockliffe, S. (1985) *The Experience of Residential Care from the Perspective of Children and Parents and Caregivers*, Report to the ESRC, University of York.